:

Paris

A guide to recent architecture

D1357897

Paris

● ● ● ellipsis K Ö N E M A N N

Barbara-Ann Campbell

A guide to recent architecture

Barbara-Ann Campbell 1997

CREATED, EDITED AND DESIGNED BY
Ellipsis London Limited
55 Charlotte Road London EC2A 3QT
E-MAIL ...@ellipsis.co.uk
WWW http://www.ellipsis.co.uk
PUBLISHED IN THE UK AND AFRICA BY
Ellipsis London Limited
SERIES EDITOR Tom Neville
EDITOR Vicky Wilson
SERIES DESIGN Jonathan Moberly
LAYOUT Pauline Harrison

COPYRIGHT © 1997 Könemann
Verlagsgesellschaft mbH
Bonner Str. 126, D-50968 Köln

PRODUCTION MANAGER Detlev Schaper
PRINTING AND BINDING Sing Cheong Printing Ltd
Printed in Hong Kong, China

ISBN 3 89508 642 8 (Könemann)
ISBN 1 899858 05 9 (Ellipsis)

10 9 8 7 6 5 4 3 2

Contents

Introduction

Central Paris, with a population of 1.6 million, is encircled by the périphérique, the eight-lane motorway that runs on the line of the outermost of the concentric city walls (now marked by ring roads). These have radiated out from the central island, Ile de la Cité, since the third century BC – the first city 'wall' being a moat. Beyond the périphérique stretch the *banlieues* (suburbs) which comprise greater Paris, containing a population of 7 million.

There are 20 *arrondissements* in Paris, spiralling clockwise outwards from the Ile de la Cité. These municipal districts, each with its own mayor and town hall, are important administrative and topological entities. As with most cities, some neighbourhoods or *quartiers* are known more familiarly by their unofficial titles, for instance Beaubourg and Les Halles. La Défense approximates a twenty-first *arrondissement*, though it is in fact an island development outside the city walls, easily reached by road, métro or more speedily by the RER train.

At the périphérique, in the zone between the *banlieues* and the city, are tracks of industrial shedlands. Here you will find a collection of large-scale buildings such as Gaudin's Stade Sébastien-Charléty, Piano's Centre Commercial Bercy II, or Perrault's *hôtel industriel* caught in the spaghetti of motorway off-ramps. The gates to the city, once 52 Ledoux-designed *barrières* (toll-gates) along the Fermiers Généraux wall, are now transport interchanges – heliports (see the finance ministry by Chemetov and Huidobro or Aquaboulevard by Ghiulamila) and railway stations (Gare du Nord for the Eurostar) as well as the virtual gates (screens) of information interchanges such as Minitel or the Internet.

The labyrinthine transport infrastructure of Paris climbs above, dives below, weaves between and cuts through the city fabric. New infrastructure has reordered the city in each era. The dense accretion of medieval dwellings, sinuous streets and alleys that grew up in rings around the Seine was parcelled up between the axial boulevards designed by Haussmann in the nineteenth century to connect important buildings and monuments. In the twentieth century the linking of points within the city has been taken over by the subterranean rail lines of the métro and RER.

The waterways, road and rail systems each provides an important orienting route: the meandering Seine and the straightened curves of the Canal St-Martin which branches north-east towards La Villette; the Champs-Elysées axis striking north-west from Le Nôtre's Tuileries Gardens at the Louvre, under the Arc de Triomphe out to the Grande Arche at La Défense; and Métro Line 1 which crosses Paris underground on the same trajectory. Place de la Bastille operates as a fulcrum for all three. From these routes one's position in the city can be referenced.

The Seine divides the city roughly in half, into areas north and south of the river, referred to as the right and left banks. The banks are stitched together by bridges both to look at and look from. Mimram's Passerelle Solférino is being constructed, and the choreographed lighting of Pont de Bir-Hakeim will soon be unveiled. Other key orientation and surveillance points are the *places*, from which star-bursts of roads issue outwards. Here buildings such as Tange's Grand Ecran at place d'Italie or Ott's Opéra at place de la Bastille occupy landmark positions.

The historic *quartiers* of the city are being darned together in ways that protect the ecology and culture of the local communities. The repaving of the winding backstreets around rue Montorgueil by Drummond is exemplary. Passage Brady – typical of the glass-roofed Parisian arcades – is being renovated by Lemoine. The sector Goutte d'Or is a test case of restoration and the integration of new projects, while the undecided fate of the ZAC des Amandiers' dwellings in Ménilmontant is attracting

Paris: a guide to recent architecture

international attention thanks to the protests of Claire Robinson and Archi xxe.

Of the city's unbuilt projects, one of the most influential has been Rem Koolhaas' 1993 Jussieu Library competition entry. Koolhaas envisaged a building at once a continuation of the centreless grid of the existing Jussieu campus and a counterpoint to it. The university court is spun into a ramp, comparable to the public space of a city, interconnecting individual libraries of a more transient nature. This 'warped interior boulevard' creates a 'vertical intensified landscape', the talk of contemporary architecture schools. The project is published in Koolhaas' megatome SMLXL.

Paris has a structuring landscape of historic and modern monuments. Historic monuments include the Eiffel Tower, the Louvre Palace, the Musée d'Orsay and the Viaduc Daumesnil – civil engineering from the graduates of the Grande Ecole des Ponts et Chaussées. Plans for buildings protected under the description *monument historique* (including pieces as diverse as Notre Dame and the banks of the Seine) and for any building within 500 metres of a listed building must be submitted for approval by the Architectes des Bâtiments de France, where the project is vulnerable to refusal, sometimes without explanation.

The modern monuments are mostly the *grands projets*. Since de Gaulle, French presidents have tended to concentrate their monumental works in Paris. Pompidou commissioned the arts centre that bears his name. Giscard d'Estaing attempted to build a large monument designed by Ricardo Bofill on the site of the old market, Les Halles, but mayor Chirac (fortunately) stopped it. At the time of his defeat by Mitterrand, Giscard d'Estaing had initiated two more monuments in Paris: the Parc and Cité des Sciences at La Villette and the Musée d'Orsay. Mitterrand decided to maintain both projects, and added a few of his own: the restructuring of the Louvre, the new finance ministry at Bercy, the Institut du Monde Arabe, the people's opera house at Bastille and the Grande Arche at La Défense. Mitterrand's projects were started in haste as there were fears that the socialists would not survive the 1986 elections. As it happened, he was re-elected and proceeded to commission the Cité de la Musique and the Bibliothèque de France to round off his *œuvre complète*.

The *grands projets* are undoubtedly the best-known competitions outside France. But nationally there has been considerable support for young practices. PAN (new architecture programme) annually invites architects to submit work which is considered for various awards and the winning names added to circulated local-authority listings. The Ministère de l'Urbanisme et du Logement publishes the work of selected architects in the *Albums de la Jeune Architecture* – prestigious small catalogues the architects can give to prospective clients.

Competition-winning designs for local-authority programmes are put out to tender. The successful tenderer, usually a large contractor or spec-ulative developer, accepts both design and architect as part of the contract. Thus the client is also the builder, which means cost-cutting is invariably an issue. The battle to control the quality of the detailing is made more difficult by the French practice of using *bureaux d'études*, working-drawing offices generally employed by the developer/contractor. While some practices, such as Simounet, have done their own high-quality detailing in-house, there is an absence of the tradition of detailing that exists elsewhere in Europe. It could be argued that the *bureaux d'études* have as much influence on architecture as have the architects themselves.

Part of the context in which the built environment of Paris must be considered is the education of its architects. After the student riots of '68, the Beaux Arts educational model – that had reigned unchallenged for 150 years – was rejected and a new structure of UPS (Unités Pédagogiques) set up. The eight UPS were independent and state financed. Each became known for a different concern: social housing, building technology, social sciences, space manipulation, and so on. UP6 was the hotbed of activism and conflict continued for a further two years until several teachers and their students decamped to UP8. By the mid 1970s these two schools were the most important in France, both preoccupied with the recovery of French urbanism.

The role of the media has also been crucial. The research coming out of the UPS was at first published under the enlightened editorship of Bernard Huet in *Architecture d'Aujourd'hui*, alongside the work of well-known foreign architects. This started to break down French insularity and introduce young architects to a wider discourse. The other important laboratory is CERA (Centre d'Etudes et de Recherche Architecturale), where sophisticated historical investigations provide theoretical bases for design hypotheses.

Many of the better housing projects, often designed by young teams, have been sponsored by SEM (Société d'Economie Mixte). RIVP (Régie Immobilière de la Ville de Paris) is an enlightened 'mixed-finance' developer which invests 50:50 public and private money. This system protects tenants with subsidised rents. In 1990 the Ministère des Postes et Télé-communications initiated a programme to optimise the use of its sites. These projects, accommodating a total of 1500 employees and usually with a post office included in the brief, were often entrusted to young architects such as Bourdeau and Borel.

Re-use is a city theme. Notable re-uses in Paris include the multi-storey carpark turned into offices by Canal, the abattoir that became the Cité des Sciences et de l'Industrie, and the train shed that became the museum of nineteenth-century art, Musée d'Orsay. The disappearance of industrial buildings and transport networks has also created space in certain areas for large-scale masterplanning and development schemes to assist in the regeneration of the city, for example, Allée Darius-Milhaud by Sarfati/AREA which occupies a decommissioned railway route. Many of these have been studied by APUR (Atelier Parisien d'Urbanisme) and recommendations made. ZACS (Zones d'Aménagement Concertées) are designated areas of mixed-use development within which purpose-designed planning regulations apply. They are usually masterplanned by an architect who then co-ordinates the selection of other architects for different projects. In addition to the ZAC Citroën-Cévennes on the site of a former Citroën factory and the ZAC de Bercy on the site of former wine warehouses, the ZAC Seine Rive Gauche around the new Bibliothèque de France, at 150 hectares one of the largest redevelopments, will radically change the character of this part of Paris.

Underground developments such as the commercial catacombs around Pei's Pyramide Inversée, Piano's IRCAM and Chemetov's extension to Les Halles present solutions to the spatial claustrophobia of the city. Looked at in conjunction with the modernisation of the sewers and the métro system, it appears that redevelopments, including large chunks of city with streets and squares, are now being pursued below ground.

Back in the open, the parks of Paris range from the spinney of silver birches planted by Desvignes et Dalnoky inside Piano's housing scheme on rue du Meaux and Berger's linear garden carried on Viaduc Daumesnil, to the vast masterplanned expanses of Tschumi's Parc de la Villette and the park ZAC of Berger, Viguier and Jodry at Parc André-Citroën. Gardens

Paris: a guide to recent architecture

within gardens have become a theme: the Jardin des Bambous by Chemetoff within La Villette; the Jardin Noir by Provost and the Jardin Sériel by Clément within Parc André-Citroën. The newly designed pylons by Mimram and Ritchie/RFR/Gustafson are man-made 'trees' in the ultimate park: the countryside beyond the périphérique.

Walking between projects you will be seduced by the street furniture that contributes so much to the culture of Paris: the cast-iron tree gratings reinterpreted by Mangin-Seura/Osty on boulevard Richard-Lenoir, sculptures such as Les Colonnes de Buren, Decaux's ubiquitous toilet pod, Foster's bus stop on the Champs-Elysées axis as well as the chairs that enliven insignificant café façades, exemplified by Philippe Starck's designs for the late Café Costes.

Part of Paris' modern city image is to do with hygiene. The streetscape is biologically active, with sweepers in eco-green jumpsuits riding poop-sucking bubble-mobiles and muscley motorbikes with vacuum-cleaner attachments.

Paris is a collective masterpiece, a city of in-between spaces. The theatre is around you: the conversations beyond your café table, the Twingos on the boulevard, the cobbled alley with its concierge, the flower-seller on the steps of the cathedral, a shrug … from President Chirac.

The axis of this book begins with a pyramid, spirals outwards, and ends with a cube.

ACKNOWLEDGEMENTS

Thank you to all the architects and designers who generously supplied material; to all the architectural periodicals whose documentation of the last ten years has been invaluable; to Rory Lange, who patiently spent weeks walking around Paris with me discussing the ideas for this guide; to my teaching partner Nasrine Seraji for our hours of discussions; to Irénée Scalbert for his reading of the text and insightful comments; and to Sophie Le Bourva, M. and Mme Le Bourva and Christophe Tardy who provided an introduction to French culture, intellectual and gastronomic.

Thank you also to: Frances Anderton, Claire Robinson, Andrés F.-Atela, Jacques Sautereau, Jean Attalie, Jean-François Blassel and Amanda Johnson, Henry Bardsley, Aileen Smith, and the students of AA Diploma Unit 1, 1993–96.

My appreciative thanks to the ellipsis team for their ingenuity and tolerance: Vicky Wilson, Tom Neville, Jonathan Moberly, the sparkly Armelle Tardiveau and the maverick photographer, Keith Collie.

And especially my family, particularly Meg Campbell, George Campbell, Rob Anderson, Eileen Roberts, and Janet and Lucy.

BAC January 1997

Paris: a guide to recent architecture

Using this book

Buy the pocket 'A-to-Z', *Paris par Arrondissement*, available from book-shops and newsagents, which includes maps for streets, métros and buses.

The Paris métro is clean and efficient. Each line is designated by a number as well as by the names of the termini. The RER lines, which run through Paris and into the suburbs, can shortcut lengthy métro rides. The bus allows one to see more of the city, though it can be slow.

Bus, métro and RER all use the same tickets (one ticket per journey) as long as it is within central Paris. It is possible to buy one-, three- or five-day Paris-Visite tickets from main railway or main métro stations as well as a weekly ticket (*Coupon Hebdomadaire Jaune*), and a monthly pass (*Carte Orange*) which requires a passport-sized photo. *Carnets* of ten tickets can be purchased at any métro station and work out cheaper than individual tickets. Tickets should be retained until the end of the journey as they may be needed to operate an exit or interchange turnstile. The métro runs from about 5.30 to 1.15.

For further information on French architecture visit IFA at 8 rue de Tournon, 6e. The Pavillon de l'Arsenal at 21 boulevard Morland, 4e, has an excellent exhibition of recent projects. The best books about Parisian architecture and design are to be found at the Centre Pompidou book-shop, the Moniteur bookshops at 7 place de l'Odéon, 6e, and 17 rue d'Uzès, 2e, and La Hune, boulevard St Germain, 6e.

Paris is a walkable city. Travelling on foot from one piece of architecture to another, something will catch your eye: a wrought-iron balcony, a rippling zinc bar, or simply the gestures of a gendarme directing traffic. And then, as Ian Nairn observed in his guide to Paris of 1968, the magic will begin to work, 'and may not stop until you are drunk with a hundred patches of gravel and a thousand expressive shrugs'.

Paris: a guide to recent architecture

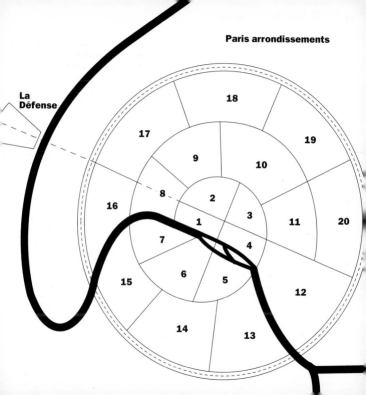

Paris arrondissements

La Défense

Louvre to Les Halles

Pyramide du Louvre

Modernisation of the Louvre was both essential and unimaginable. The 800-year-old stone palace, home to virtually every French king since 1202, was fundamentally ill-suited to serve as a museum. With only a fraction of the support space now considered mandatory for museums, the Louvre was a 'theatre with no backstage'.

This, perhaps the greatest of all the *grands projets* initiated by Mitterrand, has three distinct parts. First, the creation of a huge underground building of more than 45,000 square metres providing new technical and support facilities, doubling the exhibition space and adding public amenities. Second, the implementation of a network of pedestrian and vehicular routes which has turned the Louvre, previously a half-mile obstacle to surface circulation, into a vast interchange (at airport scale) connecting the city above and below ground. Third, the need for a new entrance has generated a landmark – the glass pyramid.

The radical nature of Pei's proposition, coupled with its prohibitive cost, was political dynamite. On the one hand it would immortalise the president more effectively than any tomb in Père-Lachaise; on the other, if this new project were seen to be the desecration of a national treasure, it could, with a little media fanning, turn public opinion against the government. A provocative article in *Le Monde* by the minister of culture proclaimed that entry to a palace via its basement was unfitting. It was decided to test the proverbial waters by mocking up Pei's pyramid at full scale.

The problem then was how to simulate a building of such proportions. The solution, arrived at in consultation with engineer Peter Rice, was to create a stretchy Kevlar cable structure covered with plastic film tensioned from its tip by a 500-tonne crane. This avoided placing a supporting post in the centre which would have destroyed the geometric and spatial purity

I M Pei and Partners 1993

I M Pei and Partners 1993

Louvre to Les Halles

of the form. The mock-up was unveiled in the early hours of an autumn morning before an audience made up of the great and the good of France. Confidence increased and viewing was extended to the public for a further three weeks. Lowered when the crane driver went home at night, it was a working-hours-only model.

For construction of the pyramid proper, the solid bars of its stainless-steel structure were welded in place and then extended by a network of extremely thin tension and compression members. Connecting the assembly are hand-crafted nodes, desirable sculptural objects, which were cast in a lost-wax process, with a two-phase blasted finish. All of these fittings were produced by a Massachusetts firm that specialises in riggings for America Cup yachts.

The structure's exact geometric position was determined through a series of sensitive tensioning operations. An iron bar was suspended from each juncture to simulate the anticipated weight of the glass skin. As each glass panel was installed, the corresponding dead-weight bar was severed. Thus throughout the operation uneven distortion stresses were avoided.

The laminated 'white' glass is sealed with structural silicon. Each panel has an aluminium frame whose minimal mullions, set flush with the glazed surface, are precisely engineered to preserve the planarity of the crystalline prism. Unlike commercially available glass, in which iron oxides cast a noticeably green tint, the pyramid's cladding is colourless glass, permitting the Louvre's honey-coloured façades to be seen without distortion.

The *petites pyramides* are a pity: a dreadful 'boom, boom' after the punchline. Worth seeing are the mountain-climbing window cleaners – now machines – that abseil down the sheer surfaces of this glass cathedral on Tuesdays, when the museum is closed.

I M Pei and Partners 1993

I M Pei and Partners 1993

Don't leave before wandering within the western end of the Tuileries Gardens, described by Ian Nairn as '... enchanted groves for world-citizens, where each gesture has its own weight and space: absolute, unimpeded by any outside influence: assessed by its own nature and no other – whether it is a kiss or a system of philosophy. This apparent innocence is in fact the product of complete sophistication, the far end of experience where everything is real and new yet full of illusion and continually remembered. Not bad for a thick copse and some gravel.'

The Tuileries Gardens are being renovated by landscape architects Pascal Criber and Louis Benech. The eastern end of Le Nôtre's symmetrical composition of geometrically patterned planted beds will be unbalanced – invisibly – by different fragrances on either side of its centre line.

ADDRESS Place du Carrousel, 1er
CLIENT Etablissement Public du Grand Louvre
ASSOCIATED ARCHITECT Michel Macary
ARCHITECTE EN CHEF DU PALAIS DU LOUVRE Georges Duval
STRUCTURAL ENGINEER concrete/steel Fred Storksen, SEEE (for Dumez)
ARCHITECTURAL CONCRETE Jean-Pierre Aury (for Dumez)
PYRAMID STRUCTURE DESIGN CONCEPT Nicholet Chartrand Knoll, Ltd
CONTRACTORS foundations, Quillery; pyramid, CFEM; civil engineering, Dumez
CONSTRUCTION COST Grand Louvre FF1,100 million (projected)
GROSS BUILDING AREA Grand Louvre 90,000 square metres
METRO Palais-Royal/Louvre
ACCESS open every day except Tuesday. Permanent collections open 9.00–18.00, temporary exhibitions open 10.00–22.00

I M Pei and Partners 1993

I M Pei and Partners 1993

Louvre to Les Halles

Pyramide Inversée

The Pyramide Inversée marks the underworld threshold between commercial catacombs and museum. If the Grande Pyramide symbolises the entrance to the Louvre from above ground, the Pyramide Inversée is the entrance for Paris' troglodyte shoppers and car-parkers.

The Pyramide Inversée turns the structure upside down: its apex is its lowest point. Above ground the 'base' is all but invisible, suggesting a pool glinting in the undergrowth of a busy roundabout. Its deliberate lack of presence ensures an uninterrupted view from the Arc du Carrousel to the entrance of the Grande Pyramide.

The Peter Rice-designed structure is equally paradoxical. No canonical catalogue solutions. Polished precipitation-hardened stainless steel throughout, it uses the deflections of the system to advantage. Sparse connections to nodes solve technical problems without major contortions and requiring minimal on-site adjustment.

The skylight base and the inverted pyramid are structurally independent, though both are tensioned against a 30-tonne, 13.3-metre-square steel caisson frame working on the principle of a piano frame – the heavier the frame, the longer the wires stay in tune. All the triangular glass faces of the pyramid are hung. Spherical bearings centre the loads on the glass, which is hung from springs at the top. Each panel is picked up at its centre by a fine cable linked to a flying post. These flying posts, eight solid steel rods which also act as counterweights to stop the pyramid swaying, are supported by cables which tie back to the edge beam. The lightness of this structure is possible because of the weight of the glass which counters wind-pressure load reversal.

A small limestone pyramid prevents passage and possible impaling beneath the point. This can be moved and the bottom four panels unclipped – like a glass lotus flower – and cradled out of the way. Its heart

I M Pei, Pei Cobb Freed and Partners; Michel Macary 1993

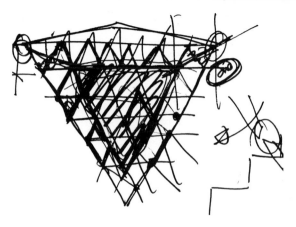

I M Pei, Pei Cobb Freed and Partners; Michel Macary 1993

Louvre to Les Halles

is empty of structure to allow the insertion of a scaffolding tower. Positive-pressure, warm, dry, filtered air is trickle fed in through the edge frame to avoid condensation and keep the inside clean.

The 30-mm-thick water-white glass is tempered laminated float, bright annealed only in the base. The edges are cut at an angle and then polished. On the base, the triple-laminate panels are cut in kissing chamfers with silicon butt-jointing the kiss. On the faces, the double-laminate lozenge panes are cut in parallel skew chamfers using a universal edge geometry algorithm throughout, formed by the intersection of the vertical construction planes with the sloping faces. Here there is no silicon.

Pei's team was aware from the start of the prismatic potential of these edges. As the sun strikes, the colourless glass breaks the spectrum into ochres, viridians and ultramarines across the floor, empurpling the limestone. A frieze of spotlights between the pyramid and its base uses mirrors to bounce light up and down, animating the structure after dark.

Tip poised 1.4 metres above the floor, the pyramid lantern hangs directly in one's field of vision, a crystalline periscope where light, image and shadow ricochet into a multiple-exposure diorama. Standing still, one experiences a series of viewing positions, a kaleidoscopic layering of floor, wall, structure and sky, magical as virtual people march vertically up the glass seams. Make an appointment an hour before sunset.

ADDRESS Palais du Louvre, 1er
CLIENT Etablissement Public du Grand Louvre
BET structure, RFR
CONTRACTOR METAL STRUCTURE Eiffel
METRO Palais-Royal/Louvre
ACCESS open 9.00–18.00

I M Pei, Pei Cobb Freed and Partners; Michel Macary 1993

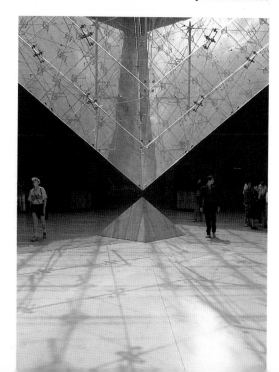

Richelieu Wing

The nineteenth-century Richelieu Wing of the Louvre lies between the Cour Napoléon and Percier and Fontaine's marching arcades on the rue de Rivoli. It was vacated in 1989 by the finance ministry for Chemetov and Huidobro's *grand projet* megalith in Bercy (see page 146). Eight administrative levels have become three airy floors of museum space with the three internal courtyards transformed from civil-servant carparks to covered sculpture courts. Two specialist teams of engineers, both under Peter Rice's leadership, were commissioned to design light-filtering roofs for the wing: one to design the structure, the other the natural lighting.

The courtyards have irregularly tapering plans, their width reducing from 41 to 28 metres. The transparent roofs – finely screened with aluminium rods – are shallow vaults with hipped ends, their height limited to preserve the Louvre's roofline silhouette. These courtyard umbrellas are propped off the cornices by series of short vertical posts, allowing smoke outlets to be hidden beneath their eaves. They hover.

The second kind of new roof belongs to the top floor of the wing, remodelled to take advantage of natural overhead light. The criteria which govern this new skylighting system balance conservation considerations necessary to protect the paintings with the viewing conditions desired by the public. Paris daylight was studied: at different times during the day, throughout the year and in different weather conditions. To minimise the variations, the skylight system was designed as three layers, allowing only diffused sunlight to enter.

The first layer is of glass rooflights which incorporate an ultra-violet filtering laminate. Despite the slight colour shift towards green, the additional cost of 'white' low-iron glass could not be justified.

The second sun-screen layer is a matt-white egg-crate louvre made of aluminium blades installed immediately beneath the glass. Direct sunlight

I M Pei, Pei Cobb Freed and Partners; Michel Macary 1992

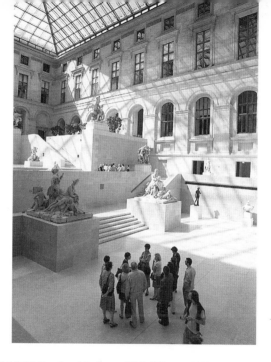

I M Pei, Pei Cobb Freed and Partners; Michel Macary 1992

must not land on the paintings at any time, so the dimensions and depth of the screen were calculated for the exact orientation and gradient of each rooflight.

A third light-directing layer of white-painted plaster blades directs light from the rooflights to the gallery walls. The form of the blades was developed to allow the walls to receive light directly from the underside of the sun screen, while ensuring that in most cases the floor was obscured. These also conceal the banks of fluorescent tubes which supplement daylight when necessary.

The hardest criterion was 'to maintain contact with the external environment'. Pei wanted a clear view through the rooflights of clouds, blue sky and weather conditions, so no diffusing glass was allowed and the sun screens were designed to enable vistitors to look up and see the sky.

In addition to computer models, a full-scale mock-up was built in the Tuileries Gardens to allow curators to experiment with the light. Priceless paintings were brought from the museum to add realism in a unique Louvre-privileged scenario.

ADDRESS Palais du Louvre, 1er
CLIENT Etablissement Public du Grand Louvre
CONSULTING ENGINEER Ove Arup & Partners
GLAZING SUBCONSULTANT Ian Ritchie with RFR
BUREAU DE CONTROLE Véritas
CONTRACTORS steel, Viry; glazing, Dutemple
SIZE 22,000 square metres
METRO Grand-Palais/Louvre
ACCESS open every day except Tuesday, 9.00–18.00

I M Pei, Pei Cobb Freed and Partners; Michel Macary 1992

I M Pei, Pei Cobb Freed and Partners; Michel Macary 1992

Colonnes de Buren

An active 1980s public arts programme in Paris has spawned the numerous murals and sculptures that lurk elevated on *pignons* (gable walls) and at cross-routes. Few are good. Most have a simplistic energy which either fails to compete with billboard sophistication, or remains a half-remembered background presence despite being at an unoverlookable scale.

For the courtyard of the Palais-Royal, the plague of cars has been banished and artist Daniel Buren invited to perform. An artist of considerable stature, his work is site specific. An assortment of stripy liquorice columns stomps across the court in circus parade (night-lit with strips of airfield runway lights). The effect imitates, with delightful precision, the rhythm of the double colonnade (Pierre Fontaine, 1829) which screens the lawn of gravel, marching arcades, stripy awnings and columnar box-pruned trees of the garden of the Palais-Royal beyond.

Commissioned by the minister of culture, Buren's columns caused a national uproar. They are positioned on the roof of a new subterranean conference suite whose cambered construction raised the ground level, distorting (to the sensitive eye) the proportions and balance of the palace façades. After the March 1986 elections Buren's project ran into trouble when its FF7-million cost was revealed. Buren promptly took out an injunction against the new minister of culture, arguing that French law entitles artists to complete commissioned work, which must not be judged until it is finished. Enjoying no such privileges, a number of architects took up the cause, among them Christian de Portzamparc, Jean Nouvel and Bernard Tschumi. However, the artist's legal status in France was never tried, as Buren was given the go-ahead.

Buren's columns divide public opinion. But on closer examination the conflict has less to do with the project itself than with its location. Paris-

Daniel Buren 1986

Daniel Buren 1986

ians are extremely fond of the Palais-Royal, from whose gardens on 13 July 1789 Camille Desmoulins delivered the inflammatory speech that precipitated the storming of the Bastille the following day. Rather than segregating contemporary art from historic monuments, it would seem a sensible compromise to assign a sell-by date.

ADDRESS courtyard of Palais-Royal, 1er
CLIENT Ministère de la Culture
CONTRACT VALUE FF7 million
METRO Palais-Royal
ACCESS open

Daniel Buren 1986

Louvre to Les Halles

Daniel Buren 1986

Underground complex at Les Halles

The original market was designed by Victor Baltard and Félix Callet in 1869 – a stunning set of square iron-and-glass pavilions connected by covered streets along which ran streams of water below open-work gratings. These elegant sheds were deserted a hundred years later when the vegetable and meat markets moved to the suburbs. This left a central area ripe for development and a consortium of vested interests was set up to supervise a commercial strategy.

The money spinning revolved around a major new rail interchange where two new RER routes would link into the four existing métro lines. This required deep open-cast excavation, so the delicate glassy pavilions stood no chance of survival. The 1971 demolition began deviously in August, when most Parisians are away on holiday, and by 1974 there was nothing left save one rescued pavilion now orphaned in the suburbs.

The in-fighting continued, now over a gaping hole. The substructure of sewers and services charged ahead, but the ground-level image could not be agreed on, except for the Forum, a shopping complex with a sunken courtyard, for which Penchreac'h and Vasconi were commissioned in 1973. With the election of President Giscard d'Estaing in 1974 a new approach was sought. Proposals were commissioned, first from Ricardo Bofill, then from three teams of architects, one of which included Bofill, finally from a series of architects invited to work in partnership – still including Bofill. A scheme was at last selected and work had started when in 1977 Chirac was elected the first mayor of Paris since 1870.

There then ensued a struggle between president and mayor over the future of the site. Chirac won, and the Bofill project was abandoned. The final result comprises the busy RER/métro interchange, the tacky Penchreac'h and Vasconi Forum and an expansion of this by Penchreac'h and Manoïlesco, next to Chemetov's underground sports complex.

Paul Chemetov 1985

Louvre to Les Halles

Louvre to Les Halles

Paul Chemetov 1985

Entry/exits to the underworld are via escalators. As elsewhere in Paris, one is served up on to the pavement. The Centre Pompidou zig-zag, the umbilical travelators at Châtelet and the strong, springy and stepless experience of the doughnut hole at Roissy airport make Paris the escalator capital of Europe. Escalators have an elegance that lifts lack.

Chemetov's complex, the first of the underground *quartiers* built in Paris, lies 20 metres below the lacklustre public gardens of Les Halles. With its Olympic-sized swimming pool and winter garden, the huge underground area is a new piece of city, with streets and squares and a massive concrete skeleton on the scale of a cathedral.

The main nave leads to a five-storey square. The complex is simply organised around three underground streets, concentrating on the lofty 10-metre-wide Grande Galerie which divides the shopping mall from the public utilities of swimming pool, gymnasia and *videothèque*, as well as connecting the main squares. The Grande Galerie is a particularly successful space, dramatised at points by opening up to natural light. Less successful are some of the metal métro-carriage details, including the cumbersome suspended lighting system in the main gallery, and the fact that the centre of the passage is taken up by columns rather than people.

Louvre to Les Halles

ADDRESS under the garden of Les Halles, entrances on rue Rambuteau and rue Berger, 1er
CLIENT Ville de Paris
METRO Les Halles/Châtelet-Les-Halles
ACCESS open

Paul Chemetov 1985

Paul Chemetov 1985

Café Costes

The late Café Costes deserves to be remembered for two things besides its clientèle: its chairs and its toilets.

Chairs in Paris spill out of cafés, redefining the edge of buildings. A corner café will, during its working hours, arrange outdoors an undulating skirt of chairs and tables, a shifting landscape fluttering and cluttering in response to climates meteorological and conversational. Particularly wonderful about the Café Costes chairs was the way they appeared to be talking to one another before they were occupied.

The chairs work architecturally at three scales: *en masse* they form a temporary territorial extension to the building; in groups of three or four they compose virtual rooms of space; individually they are examples of an intelligently detailed structure in which materials are employed for what they do best. The bent-ply back, structurally stiff, angles outwards, offering space, inviting occupation, becoming curving arms to enclose without confining. The finger-hole lifting grip is both practical and decorative. The tripod metal legs are stable and the wipe-down black plastic cushion comfortable. A constructional, ergonomic and aesthetic synergy.

In the toilets transparent basins meet a mirror-wall of water against which men pee. A zig-zagging glass partition of sandblasted translucency divides *Hommes* from *Dames*. Women are disorientated by kaleidoscopic mirrors: is this a door or a wall? Expressed water pipes and water acoustics orchestrate the no-hands minimalism.

Jean-Louis Costes, youngest son of Auvergnat farmers, came to Paris in his teens. Beginning as a dishwasher, he opened Café Costes ten years later, his ambition to create the biggest café in the centre of the capital, a venue 'modern and unique for its time'. Through a serendipitous encounter, Philippe Starck was employed to design the new environment and the tradition of interior architecture for cafés was revived.

Philippe Starck 1984

Louvre to Les Halles

Philippe Starck 1984

The art of the café is to sell time. Historically, these public spaces of Paris have acted as literary salons in whose spiralling smoke, to the clinking of glasses, theories artistic, philosophical and political have been elucidated. Le Café de Flore, 6e, was famous as the stronghold of Sartre and Simone de Beauvoir, while Les Deux Magots, 6e, was embraced by the Surrealists, Picasso, Le Corbusier and James Joyce.

As we went to press Naff Naff had moved into the space and destroyed most of the interior – although the bathrooms are believed to be intact. With the demise of Café Costes, you could try Café Beaubourg, on the Pompidou piazza, modelled by Christian de Portzamparc and run by Jean-Louis' older brother, Gilbert.

Note Starck's nightclub interiors: Les Bainesdouches, 7 rue du Abbé, 3e, open 23.00 until dawn; La Cigale, 120 boulevard Rochechouard, red velvet and tilting dance floor.

Louvre to Les Halles

ADDRESS place des Innocents, 1er
METRO Châtelet-Les-Halles/Etienne Marcel

Philippe Starck 1984

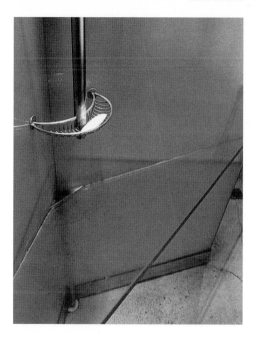

Philippe Starck 1984

Passerelle Solférino

The existing Solférino footbridge over the Seine – built in 1958 as a 'temporary' structure – has a wonderful understated presence. Simple and delicate, it is a refreshing contrast to some of its more academic neighbours. It is being replaced by a 'permanent' new bridge, designed by Ponts-et-Chaussées- (Bridges and Roadways) educated Mimram.

The competition-winning design for the footbridge beat entries by Berger, Deslaugiers, Valode et Pistre, Fuksas and Calatrava. It resolves the problem of a dominant form by dissolving the silhouette between two slender and sectionally evolving arches. These lace together the bank elevations via the two diverging and converging levels of the footbridge. The structure registers the springing steps of its travellers and has something of the presence of a large insect hovering over the water.

ADDRESS between quai Anatole France, 7e, and quai des Tuileries, 1er
CLIENT Etablissement Public du Grand Louvre/Ministère de l'Equipement, du Logement et des Transports/Ministère de la Culture et de l'Education Nationale
METRO Tuileries/Solférino/Chambre des Députés
ACCESS open

Marc Mimram, first phase 1995

Marc Mimram, first phase 1995

Pont Neuf Wrapped

Christo: While our temporary works of art all contain, at various degrees, elements of social, political, economic and environmental concerns, they also have aspects of painting, architecture, sculpture and urban planning.

Pont Neuf crosses the western extremity of Ile de la Cité, joining the left and right banks to the island – the heart of Paris for more than 2000 years. It is the oldest existing bridge in Paris, begun by Baptiste du Cerceau and completed in 1607, then changed and added to several times until 1890. It was the first bridge built without houses lining each side.

Christo and Jeanne-Claude's wrapping of the Pont Neuf in September 1985 in silky sandstone-coloured fabric commented on the tradition of successive metamorphoses of the city's bridges. Starting by persuading the people of the neighbourhood to agree to their project, their ten-year campaign for its realisation continued all the way to the mayor and the president. Exposure and controversy are effective means of generating interest and funds. The bridge was transformed for 14 days into a work of art – not least the work and art of negotiations and permissions for temporary constructions – during which time it continued to be used.

ADDRESS Pont Neuf, 1er
ENGINEER USA engineers, Theodore Dougherty
CLIENTS Ville de Paris, Ministère de la Seine et d'Etat
CONTRACTOR Charpentiers de Paris, Gérard Moulin
COST all expenses borne by the artist
SIZE 40,876 square metres of fabric, 13 kilometres of rope
MÉTRO Pont Neuf
ACCESS gone

Louvre to Les Halles

Christo and Jeanne-Claude 22 September 1985

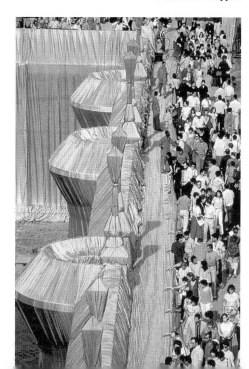

La Twingo

I think that cars today are almost the exact equivalent of the great Gothic cathedrals: I mean the supreme creation of an era, conceived with passion by unknown artists, and consumed in image if not in usage by a whole population which appropriates them as a purely magical object.
'The New Citroën' from *Mythologies* by Roland Barthes

In the beginning Archigram invented the 'Cushicle' (1966–67), a nomadic unit envisaged as part of an urban system of serviced personalised enclosures. Its compact curves predate the Twingo, a cheeky box-on-wheels.

The Twingo performs in Parisian circulation as a svelt moving container. A design that breaks all the rules of a market where economic restrictions are invariably used to justify a lack of imagination, this is a life-style accessory that happens to be a mode of transport. Dashboard signage and big-button video-game controls give the come-on. So far she has been engineered for left-hand drive only.

ENGINE 1.2 litre
FUEL CONSUMPTION 38.17 mpg (urban cycle); 55.41 mpg (at 56 mph); 40.35 mpg (at 75 mph)
FUEL SUPPLY electronic monopoint injection (Magneti Marelli)
EXHAUST three-way catalytic convertor with oxygen sensor
SIZE length 3433 millimetres, width 1633 millimetres, height 1423 millimetres; ground clearance 120 millimetres
WEIGHT 790 kg unladen
PERFORMANCE 0–63.5 mph in 14 seconds
MAXIMUM SPEED 93.75 mph

Renault 1993

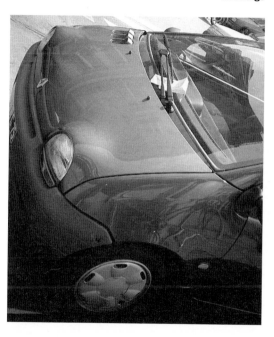

Louvre to Les Halles

Renault 1993

Sentier to Marais

Montorgueil-St-Denis pedestrian area

> Roads no longer merely lead to places, they *are* places.
> J B Jackson, *A Sense of Place, A Sense of Time*, 1994

This medieval area has been darned together with one of the most elegant and modest pedestrian renovations to be seen anywhere in the city.

The project centres on rue Montorgueil, last survivor of Zola's *Le Ventre de Paris*. At the lower end of the street, fruit, flower and cheese markets spill on to the pavement. Ficelles and baguettes of categorised lengths and diameters are stacked timber-merchant style in patisserie windows. The famous *Puits d'Amour*, a speciality of former proprietor Bourdaloue, can be found at Patisserie Stöhrer (1730, with coat-of-arms). Cafés, some with their original rippling zinc bars, promise coffee and conversations. Sample the sweetbreads of the *triperies*.

Among the rag trade of rue St Denis, winking neon and plastic-strip curtains lure adults in for entertainment. Doorways frame prostitutes, while lorries delivering cloth hold up the traffic between the restaurants of the seventeenth-century *sentier*. Sex with food with architecture.

As you stroll down rue Mandar in the early morning, the road shines, newly washed by the teams of municipal street sweepers armed with parrot-green plastic fake-yew broomsticks. The street-zone surface is deftly tailored to meet the individual characteristics of each door, step and shop threshold: remarkable on-site craftsmanship by those who cut and laid these miles of stone. The bellied road glints lightly (stunning in the rain), its swirling mosaic of square white hand-laid marble fragments set in arcs described by the swing of an arm. It is a delicate contrast to the usual curb-to-curb carpet of bitumen. Catch a sighting of the remote-controlled bollards descending into their underworld.

At dusk, stand on the steps where rues Montmartre, Montorgueil and

Didier Drummond 1994

Turbigo intersect, with your back to the anaesthetising emporium of the 'new' Les Halles, and look down into this sector. Rooftops, chimneys and zinc mansards glow under the sun's last rays. Narrow streets, leaning walls of shutters and balconies, clusters of chairs and stalls: here is the density and vitality of the living city, unperturbed by meandering tourists.

This project has a sensitivity of scale and detail which suggests that its author understands the difference between the life of the street and the deathliness of the mall. £15 per footstep.

ADDRESS sector bounded by rue Réaumur, boulevard Sébastopol, rue Etienne Marcel and rue du Louvre, 2e
CLIENT Ville de Paris/Direction de la Voirie
CONTRACT VALUE FF100 million
SIZE 20 hectares; total length of streets 2.3 kilometres
METRO Les Halles/Etienne Marcel/Sentier/Réaumur-Sébastopol
ACCESS open

Didier Drummond 1994

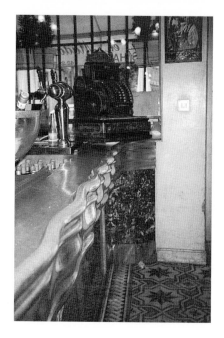

Didier Drummond 1994

Public convenience

The Decaux automatic public convenience is now a familiar sight on the streets of Europe. An autonomous repeated object distributed throughout the city, it delivers 'point-type' facilities with a succinctness and precision to rival Tschumi's follies at La Villette (see page 234).

The door opens automatically after inserting a coin in the slot, then closes and locks behind the user, to be easily opened from the inside at any time. Natural and artificial light are distributed from a circular skylight, while mirror, paper dispenser, handbasin and soap dispenser are at one's fingertips. The floor is non-slip and the cast-aluminium bowl has a fire-resistant plastic coating. After use, a strict and fully automatic cleansing cycle begins before another user is admitted. The floor is sprayed clean and the toilet retracts into a wall compartment where it too is sprayed clean, disinfected and air-dried. Special-access models have been developed with organisations representing differently-abled groups.

Decaux, a family-owned, private company, offers regular maintenance as part of the service: when a Decaux toilet malfunctions, a Decaux-mobile with a trained technician is on the spot in moments. The most taxing assignment is encouraging all parties to agree on the location of a cubicle. Visibility needs to be balanced against discretion. Then all that is required is a suitable foundation, connection to the main sewer, a water supply and electric power outlet. Compared with traditional toilets, the Decaux conveniences offer appreciable savings. Industrial-design engineering at its best: refreshing, simple, convenient.

ADDRESS all over Paris, for example, rue des Quatre Fils, 3e
CLIENT the mayor of each *arrondissement*
SIZE 1.2 X 1.94 X 2.65 metres
ACCESS open 24 hours, FF1

J C Decaux current model 1994

Musée Picasso

The meeting of art and architecture has always been problematic. How the architect resolves the movement of people within the constraints of site and budget may conflict with the artist's opinion of how his or her work should be shown. Committed collaboration is essential given that the two disciplines share certain concerns: decisions about balance, articulated in languages that deal with space-time.

Until the sixteenth century the Marais, in the 3e and 4e *arrondissements*, was a marsh. It was then flamboyantly built upon by nobility desiring proximity to the royal court at the Hôtel de Tournelles with grandiose town houses – *hôtels particuliers* – which developed a standardised *parti*. A *corps-de-logis* with narrow wings forming a courtyard was enclosed towards the street by a high wall or stable-and-kitchen block, broken by the entrance porch. Typically there would be a garden or small park behind overlooked by a first-floor gallery. Many of these *hôtels* were near ruin before being rescued by the city and renovated for public use. The Musée Picasso is located in the Hôtel Salé (originally the Hôtel Aubert de Fontenay, 1659, by Jean Bouillier), which was bought in 1964 by the Ville de Paris and declared a historic monument. The decision to turn this *hôtel particulier* into a museum housing Picasso's personal art collection, predominantly his own works, was taken in 1975.

Here Simounet (died 1996) used an approach that is conceptual and intellectual rather than physical and sensory. His long programme of work on minimal dwellings and low-cost housing provided him with technical insights still largely missing from architectural practice in France, where dependence on the *bureaux d'études* (working-drawing smithies) has left the profession without the strong tradition of detailing that exists elsewhere in Europe. Simounet's modest house in Corsica (1969) prefaces a play of light, shadow and route refined in the museum.

Roland Simounet 1985

Roland Simounet 1985

The language of cubism permitted simultaneous, seemingly incompatible viewpoints to tell several stories at once. As a container to display Picasso's work, this architectural realisation of the cubist approach – multiple views achieved via a route – vacillates between complicated knot and tangle. Fragmented rooms and room fragments provide a disorienting journey. The labyrinthine exploration begins with the grand staircase where ramps and thresholds mark the principal periods of Picasso's *œuvre*. The relatively unaltered original rooms on the upper floors and the heavy structure of the basement are welcome foils to the zones of energetically juxtaposed slots between floor edge and wall, steps in wall surfaces, boxes protruding from walls and slits in ceilings. The pleasant, naturally lit, covered sculpture court is fenced by low terraces and steps at curious angles, with a large window in one wall behind which people disappear along another strangely angled passage.

According to Le Corbusier, 'architects … like politicians, cannot be too far ahead of their moment, unlike artists'. Go and see Picasso's Picassos.

ADDRESS Hôtel Salé, 5 rue Thorigny, 3e
CLIENT Ministère de la Culture et de la
Communication/Direction des Musées de France
BET CONSULTANTS structure, Verfon Russo;
heating, Inex; acoustics, Val Conseil; lighting,
M Berne
CONTRACT VALUE FF53 million (1985)
SIZE 5458 square metres
METRO St-Paul/St-Sébastien-Froissart/Chemin-Vert
ACCESS open every day except Tuesday, 9.30–18.00

Roland Simounet 1985

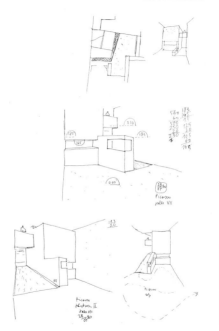

Roland Simounet 1985

Libération

Modern cities are oppressed by cars, and Paris is no exception. Place de la Bastille at rush hour is a terrifying laneless skirmish, while place de la Concorde is an eight-lane racetrack. Don't try to see the centre of Paris by car except on a Sunday, preferably in August.

Besides the jams, the noise and the fumes, like most cities Paris also suffers from the lumpen monstrosities of multi-storey carparks inherited from the 1960s. These dank concrete shelving systems, low-ceilinged, vandal-ridden, oil-trailed and under-used, often occupy prime inner-city sites. Architects have long argued that such buildings should be re-used for humans as well as vehicles, but while there is no shortage of ideas, the propositions remain unbuilt. This project is a rare exception.

A developer floated the idea of offering the top five floors of a multi-storey carpark, situated near République, for rent as office space. Not an attractive proposition given its unappealing elevation, while the redundant *in situ* car ramp presented Hobson's choice: a loss of lettable square metres, or removal, entailing expensive structural alterations. The architects nevertheless realised the potential of the space and drew it to the attention of the fast-expanding daily left-wing newspaper, *Libération*, which, in the throes of introducing computer technology, was looking for affordable new premises in town. A two-month discussion between Canal and *Libération* established the brief. This was followed by two months of detailed design work and four months of construction. Fast track.

The car ramp has become a physical and social link, spiralling between departments. Informal encounters on the ramp are encouraged, given that most interdepartmental communication is now done facelessly, by computer or telephone. The lifts, escape stairs and toilets are all contained in the central core with the ramp.

The offices occupy the former parking lanes, at half levels fed from

Daniel and Patrick Rubin (Canal) 1988

Daniel and Patrick Rubin (Canal) 1988

the ramp. They are separated from the ramp by clear glazed partitions, with outsize lettering declaring the name of the department. Everything is visible, with natural light and views shared across the main spaces. Even the darkrooms offer glimpses of Frankenstein's laboratory through Campari-red glass walls.

The spaciousness of the offices is accentuated by using the same carpeting throughout. The retention of the original coffered ceilings, now furred with acoustic foam, avoids a low ceiling-tile mask. Cables are contained in modestly sized surface-mounted ducts, with drop-down power points over workstations. The popular venue for breaks is the roof terrace and staff restaurant, with name-that-dome views over the city.

Canal has kept the conversion as simple as possible. With places for a certain number of staff cars in the remaining carpark floors below, *Libération* has been given 5000 square metres of office space in central Paris for only FF2700 per square metre.

The staff apparently like the new premises better than expected and are reputed to wire more journalistic copy than they previously did …

ADDRESS 15 rue Béranger, 3e
CONTRACT VALUE FF13.5 million
SIZE 5000 square metres
METRO République
ACCESS none

Daniel and Patrick Rubin (Canal) 1988

Daniel and Patrick Rubin (Canal) 1988

Centre Pompidou

Ideas of change and movement are intrinsic to the three façades of the Centre Pompidou. Three rectangular looms – front, back and base – are threaded with routes: the escalators convey; the ducts conduct; the large tilted piazza stages. Of these, the two sloping people routes – escalators and piazza – contrast: one an inclined horizontal plane inhabited by fire-eaters and break-dancers, the other a linear zig-zag of moving steel steps on the vertical surface of the elevation with Paris spread below. The building sits as an *objet trouvé* in and above the six-storey stone landscape of the seventeenth- to nineteenth-century *quartier*, Beaubourg.

The Piano-Rogers building – arguably the first of the *grands projets* – focused on adaptability. It had to cope with change: to the brief, to fire regulations, to budget, quality and politics. But the main idea survived remarkably uncompromised and the building attracts engagement as a university-of-the-street, not least because it looks like a giant model. Adaptability and flexibility are dependent on good management – as with all new equipment, users need to be educated in how to use their building to its best advantage.

To avoid the intimidating image of the institutional-esoteric, the architects opted to give the building a maverick persona, that of the unofficial-improvisational. The scale of the building is the scale of its parts, not the scale of the whole. The multicoloured rack of services echoes the verticality of the façades opposite, though it reaches twice their height. The result is illusory: the facility looks nothing like as tall as it is.

Pressed hard up against noisy rue du Renard, the building walls off the Marais, leaving over half the site as a quiet pedestrian piazza, buffered from the traffic. The intention to create a centre not just for tourists, but for people of the neighbourhood, has resulted in a dynamic meeting place where activities overlap in flexible, well-serviced spaces, open and acces-

Renzo Piano and Richard Rogers 1977

Renzo Piano and Richard Rogers 1977

sible, inside and out. The success of public involvement – the anticipated 5000 visitors per day has exceeded 25,000 – has taken the spectacle of the building beyond that of monumental inanimate object to one of live-performance ant heap: a permanent image of change.

The building is organised into four major zones: the piazza; the substructure; the superstructure and IRCAM (see page 72).

The substructure at street and piazza level contains large public areas: a forum, theatre, cinema, shops, reception and exhibition areas. Below this are technical and storage spaces, while under the piazza are the bus, lorry, car arrival and parking areas.

The superstructure consists of open floors which contain the major cultural activities, outdoor terraces and the administration departments. The 6-metre-wide west structural zone, facing the piazza, is for vertical and horizontal movement: escalators, lifts, escape stairs, glazed and open galleries or corridors, audio-visual screens, announcements. The 6-metre-wide east structural zone, on the roadside, contains the distinctive blue, green and orange tubing for all the mechanical services, goods lifts and fire stairs, with continuous steel balconies for ease of maintenance.

The floors have no fixed vertical interruptions to limit their users. The result is large open loft spaces, with more or less moveable partitions, serviced from both ceiling and floor. That the corridors, ducts, fire stairs, escalators, lifts, columns and bracing which normally interrupt floor space are on the outside gives the building its now clichéd inside-out appearance of clip-on/clip-off components and transparency of function.

Construction of the Centre Pompidou could be likened to that of a gothic cathedral in terms of scale and craftsmanship. Steel structures are usually made from off-the-peg standard sections, but in the case of the Centre Pompidou the massive cast-steel *gerberettes*, a cantilevered beam

Renzo Piano and Richard Rogers 1977

Renzo Piano and Richard Rogers 1977

solution invented to extend the floor plates, are handmade. These huge pieces are of solid steel, fettled after casting under the sweeping actions of a hand grinder, its carved movements still visible on their surfaces.

The joints between beam and *gerberette*, and *gerberette* and column, are pinned. The clear and simple detailing of each junction is the result of solving one problem at a time. It is worth standing directly underneath a column and looking up through the series of spaces articulated between the column and the *gerberettes*, one above another, to understand and enjoy the perfect diagram of forces. The structural system uses solid round bars for tension and hollow centrifugally cast steel tubes for compression. The wall thickness of the tubes decreases as they move up the building where they carry less load – a change in strength but not in visible size. The beams consist of a continuous double tube as top compression boom, and continuous double solid round as bottom tension boom.

Despite the socialist ideals that designed this culture-for-everyone kit-of-parts, its entirely hand-crafted realisation has ensured that there will only ever be one Centre Pompidou, the one in the Paris collection.

ADDRESS 19 rue Beaubourg and rue St-Martin, 4e
CLIENT Ministries for Cultural Affairs, Finance and Education
STRUCTURAL ENGINEER Ove Arup & Partners, Peter Rice
CONTRACTOR GTM
SIZE each floor 166 x 48 x 7 metres
METRO Châtelet/Rambuteau
ACCESS open Monday to Friday (not Tuesday) 12.00–22.00; Saturday and Sunday 10.00–22.00; free for anyone under 18 years old, and free entrance to exhibitions on Sunday from 10.00–14.00

Renzo Piano and Richard Rogers 1977

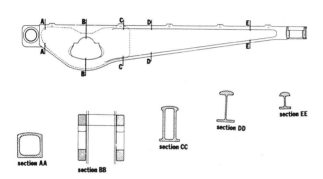

section AA

section BB

section CC

section DD

section EE

Renzo Piano and Richard Rogers 1977

IRCAM extension

Set on a busy corner, the visible tip of Piano's IRCAM building co-exists with its neighbours without over- or understatement. An extension to the subterranean network of sophisticated sound workshops designed by Piano and Rogers as part of the Centre Pompidou complex in 1977 (see page 66), its roof is the well-trodden place Igor Stravinsky, its presence unknown to sculpture-gawping pedestrians.

At the Institut de Recherche et Coordination Acoustique/Musique (IRCAM) scientists and musicians collaborate as equals in the achievement of a common goal: to abolish the boundary that separates art and science, research and creation. For a programme that sought innovative relationships between creators, musical works and the public, it was necessary to formulate a new spatial hypothesis. IRCAM is a musical instrument on an urban scale, the outcome of international, interdisciplinary research. It is not a studio, but a cluster of means and techniques necessary for physical exploration. The institute has five sections: instrumental and vocal; electro-acoustics; computing and synthesis; general acoustics; and pedagogics. In other fields, such as lighting, you can construct a 1:10 model and check what is going to happen when you transfer it to final size. In acoustics you have to work to the real scale and conditions. The experimental concert hall has a polyvalent variable volume. Acoustic combinations are multiple, from high to low frequencies, from chamber quartets to cathedral choirs. Likewise, the spatial relationship between the sources of sound and the audience can be explored.

A musical laboratory, IRCAM is set in the depths of Paris where nothing – neither air conditioning nor security systems – can disturb the atmosphere of concentration. When the institute needed to be reorganised, it was decided that the activities not requiring acoustic control should be relocated above ground, making the entire underground space available

Renzo Piano Building Workshop 1989

Renzo Piano Building Workshop 1989

to researchers. The existing area of the site, only 1 300 square metres, was maintained by taking over the former library that faces the square and building a 25-metre-high tower on a neighbouring piece of land. 'Bricks' are the only concession to traditional materials – even mortar has been dispensed with. The terracotta tiles are mechanically fixed to an aluminium frame, a strategy which allows all the benefits of prefabrication yet retains the human scale of the brick. Italianesque in its planar qualities and deep orangey-red colour, IRCAM corresponds with its neighbours – the Pompidou *gerberettes* and the gothic tracery of St-Merri – through carefully observed details. The lift-shaft tower of exposed steel carries a red-framed telephone-box glass lift. Stainless-steel doors shield access panels. A concrete bridge curves over a moat of fish-scaled, insulated glass units which let light into one of the deep rooms of this vast underground organisation.

ADDRESS place Igor Stravinsky, 4e
CLIENT Centre Georges-Pompidou/Ministère de la Culture et de la Communication
CONTRACTOR Durand Structures
BET CONSULTANTS AXE IB; GEC Ingénierie; GEMO
CONTRACT VALUE FF15 million
SIZE 5 500 square metres (2000 above ground; 3 500 underground)
METRO Châtelet/Hôtel-de-Ville/Rambuteau
ACCESS by appointment only

Sentier to Marais

Renzo Piano Building Workshop 1989

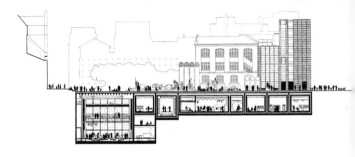

Sentier to Marais

Renzo Piano Building Workshop 1989

Apartments and gallery, rue de Venise

> Walk through rue de Venise and you'll see ... you'll see nothing!
> Jean Nouvel, award panel

Rue de Venise is a cobbled passage where seventeenth-century façades profile a sliver of Pompidou primaries. The built insertion of an apartment building and gallery is virtually invisible unless one is directly in front of it, looking up.

The shopfront showcase (plus two floors) is a designer furniture gallery. Double-height pivoting gates protect a small central recess. Above this is a one-level office and a three-floor, heavily gardened apartment. Least successful are the boxy black strip-metal balconies which attach like soap racks on the side of a bath.

The façade has a planar severity, articulated by aluminium channel-sections pressed into the pastry of glass-reinforced concrete between storey-scale panes of glass. Slipping back towards the sky, a ribbed mansard conceals a swimming pool, beside which a small terrace provides privileged views into neighbouring apartments. The finesse of the project lies in its understanding of understatement.

ADDRESS 28 rue de Venise, 4e
CLIENT SCI Venise
LANDSCAPE ARCHITECTS Michel Corajoud, David Besson-Girard
BET BTP (Niort)
BUREAU DE CONTROLE Socotec
CONTRACTOR Barbagli
SIZE 500 square metres
METRO Rambuteau
ACCESS to shop only

Serge Caillaud, with Jean-Michel Wilmotte 1990

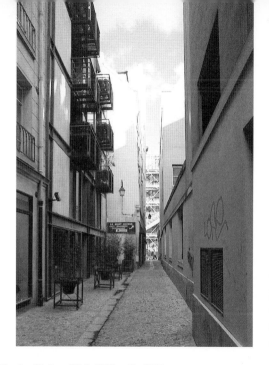

Serge Caillaud, with Jean-Michel Wilmotte 1990

Quartier Latin to Opéra

Natural History Museum

A competition in 1986 to restore, store and redisplay the museum's extensive natural-history collection – much of it the spoils of nineteenth-century expeditions – was won by the architects of the Ministry of Finance building (see page 146). The interior is like a vast high-tech aquarium of formaldehyde with the animals preserved in an antiseptic, heartless display. The skeletal cast-iron structure by Jules André (1889) houses a taxidermist's zoo alongside whale/dinosaur ribcages suspended in time beneath the 'natural' light of an artificial sky.

The foundations have been excavated to provide storage and display space and new mezzanines and bridges inserted to give informative points of view: eye to eye with a giraffe, nose to yawn with a hippo. Panoramas and close-ups are unimpeded by glass cases except from within the elevators, which carry one on a bizarre journey past stuffed exotica. Below omnivores, carnivores, herbivores and marsupials amble side by side *en train* to some out-of-sight ark.

ADDRESS 57 rue Cuvier, 5e
METAL STRUCTURE Marc Mimram
SIZE permanent exhibitions, 5000 square metres; temporary exhibitions, 1000 square metres; cultural and pedagogical centre, 1000 square metres
ACCESS open every day except Tuesday, 10.00–17.00

Paul Chemetov and Borja Huidobro 1994

Paul Chemetov and Borja Huidobro 1994

Institut du Monde Arabe

One of the most important French buildings of the 1980s and the first inspired by British high-tech, the Institut du Monde Arabe launched Nouvel's career internationally. The immediate appeal of its Swatch-watch gadgetry distracts visitors from its considered and sophisticated correspondence to the complex weave of adjacent Parisian scales. It is located amid the traditional urban density of the Faubourg St-Germain, once the aristocratic quarter where about a hundred old mansions remain, mostly housing embassies or government offices affronted by the stencilled orthogonality of the concrete Université de Jussieu. Nouvel's architecture addresses this context. The design extends in conversation, aesthetic and programmatic, conciliatory yet unfamiliar, with its surroundings.

To the roadside, the museum presents a curving shield of pressed-metal transoms rebuffing car, train and Seine. Virtually a motorway barrier, these dashing aluminium tracks make a fast corner feel faster. The lower height of the scimitar half of the building mediates between the rectangular mass behind and the scale and grandeur of boulevard St-Germain. The Cartesian library side of the institute stands in marked alignment with Albert's 1960s Faculty of Sciences, and in square *solitaire* on the grid of the Université de Jussieu.

The institute's role in the Seine-side composition has been respectfully choreographed: the rift between library and museum is on axis with the apse of Notre Dame – the *point-zéro*/centre-point of France. This narrow slot, between the tapering plan of the museum and the rectilinear library, leads to an interior mirror-paved court, veiled in wafer-thin platelets of alabaster delicately held by square paper clips. The wall power of the library side is echoed by a wide paved piazza which sets it apart from the monolithic mass of the university.

Jean Nouvel, Gilbert Lézenès, Pierre Soria, Architecture Studio 1987

Jean Nouvel, Gilbert Lézenès, Pierre Soria, Architecture Studio

The architecture engages in a series of dialectic relationships, linking and distinguishing Arab and Western culture through themes of modernity and history. Archetypal elements of traditional Arab architecture are hi-jacked: for instance, light screened through layers of frames and filters and overlaying grids. This play of light forms a backdrop to activities, a camouflage of dappled shadows, reflections and refraction. The central vertical zone of glass lifts is foil-wrapped in light metal stairs. A metaphor of movement is continued behind the transparent façade of the library where the white cylindrical book tower spirals literally, symbolically and unusefully (if pleasurably) towards heaven.

The south façade reinterprets the geometric figures and pierced openings used in Arab architecture to screen and veil. Hand-craftsmanship meets machine production through a mathematical transposition of *mouch-arabies* into an aluminium grid of 30,000 metal-petalled, photoelectrically sensitive apertures. The aesthetic unites Arab pierced sunscreen with French lace curtain in a curious and stunning indulgence of watch-making-scale technology. The furling and unfurling dilations and constrictions regulate the penetration of light like the irises of a million eyes. This magnificently romantic and decorative wall is the head-turning feature of the project, registering, quite apart from light, a major chunk of budget both upfront and in maintenance.

The launch of the competition for the Institut du Monde Arabe inaugurated Mitterrand's politically contentious policy of *grands projets*. The institute is a cross-cultural showcase: managed by the French state and 19 governments of the Arab world, it was conceived to encourage dialogue through a predominantly educational curriculum. The fabulous but spatially over-stuffed programme includes exhibition spaces, library, documentation centre and children's workshops. The museum is a trove

Jean Nouvel, Gilbert Lézenès, Pierre Soria, Architecture Studio 1987

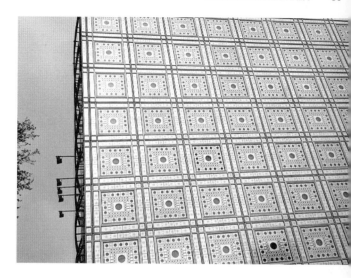

Jean Nouvel, Gilbert Lézenès, Pierre Soria, Architecture Studio

of Aladdin's Cave treasures that wink at magpie-eyed schoolchildren, while the auditorium has a polished bitumen floor and 360 extremely comfortable seats from the standard Renault car range (£100 each). One is reminded that the budget was continually cut back while construction was in progress by the many details that have prematurely lost the first flush of youth. The rooftop hosts a restaurant-café where ritzy beverages, hot and alcoholic, accompany panoramic Paris.

ADDRESS 23 quai St-Bernard, 5e
CLIENT Fondation de l'Institut du Monde Arabe
CLIENT REPRESENTATIVE SCARIF
BET CONSULTANTS building, SETEC; security, Casso et Gaudin; diaphragms, EPSI; engineer, Fruitet
SCENOGRAPHIE Jacques Le Marquet
CONTRACT VALUE FF341 million (building); FF121 million (interior fittings)
SIZE 25,263 square metres gross floor area; 16,912 square metres usable floor area
METRO Cardinal Lemoine/Jussieu/Sully-Morland
ACCESS open every day except Monday 10.00–18.00; library 13.00–20.00

Jean Nouvel, Gilbert Lézenès, Pierre Soria, Architecture Studio 1987

Jean Nouvel, Gilbert Lézenès, Pierre Soria, Architecture Studio

The result looks like a stage set for a Cecil B de Mille production of *Aïda* in which armies of palmfrond-waving slaves and elephants would triumphantly process down the central route. Such an operatic response may be partly explained also by Gae Aulenti's earlier experience in setting a Stockhausen opera in a Milan football stadium. Perhaps too it was working on a cosmic epic with Stockhausen that left her susceptible to Erich von Däniken type myths of a prehistoric machine age: if Palaeolithic space travel, why not stone steam trains – toot toot Tutankhamun.

Peter Buchanan, *Architectural Review*, December 1986

Time, tide and technology wait for no man. In Paris, vast obsolete buildings, be they train stations or abattoirs, become museums. The Gare d'Orsay, designed by Victor Laloux in 1900, was a remarkably progressive structure integrating academic classicism with advanced engineering – rivets with rosettes. Until then there had existed an architecture and engineering apartheid in railway buildings: hotels and administration quarters were privileged with self-conscious masonry grandeur, while the trains were relegated to service status beneath cast-iron sheds, out-of-sight, behind. (Compare this with the Eurostar, page 112, where the train is more sumptuously detailed than the stations.)

With a white-elephant train station one inherits a series of linear levels, tracks and platforms under a full, extruded Boullée-belly section roof. With a collection of late-nineteenth-century artworks one inherits the squabbling demands of a large homeless family of *prima donnas*. For this arranged marriage to work, it falls to the architecture of the display to mediate … and it doesn't. The design strategy is unconvincing: to lure visitors with a view of the whole space on arrival and then plunge them

Act-Architecture, Gae Aulenti 1986

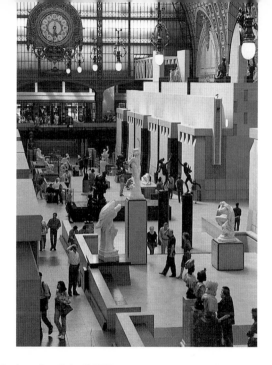

Act-Architecture, Gae Aulenti 1986

into the depths could be a legitimate orchestration of the experience, but then one would expect a similar unfolding of the display, shed and exhibits. Instead, whole views of the wonderful original interior, from the interior, are frustrated by quirkitecture. This is relieved only on ascent of a sentinel look-out tower.

The fortified Egyptian-métro arrangement to which Buchanan refers is punctuated by local stops done up in popularised architectural motifs: post-modernism as an over-friendly Muzak version of the real thing. Expensive materials are made to look cheap and tacky through their detailing and juxtaposition: the nobility of stucco is reduced to coloured plaster, while the polish and pattern of marble resembles plastic. There is a basic lack of understanding of display. The niches, pedestals, mouldings, pilasters and other details needed to mediate and introduce hierarchies of scale and integrate period settings have gone AWOL.

What hope is there to educate the general public to support quality architecture when they are led to believe, by civic investment and *grand projet* status, that this kind of stuff is good? Garnier's Opéra model and drawings are to be found here – let's hope he doesn't know.

ADDRESS 9 quai Anatole France, 7e
CLIENT Etablissement Public du Musée d'Orsay
ASSOCIATED ARCHITECTS P Colboc, R Bardon and J P Philippon
SIZE 50,000 square metres
METRO Solférino
ACCESS open Tuesday, Wednesday, Friday, Saturday 10.00–18.00;
Thursday 10.00–21.45; Sunday 9.00–18.00

Act-Architecture, Gae Aulenti 1986

Quartier Latin to Opéra

Act-Architecture, Gae Aulenti 1986

Sewer renovation

'Below Paris is another city' said Victor Hugo in *Les Misérables* (1862), referring to the sewer network, illicit pathway and seat of social pathology, vital to the gracious city above. One of Haussmann's major achievements, the sewers correspond exactly to the avenues. A formidable system laid out by the engineer Eugène Belgrand (1810–78), 2100 kilometres of galleries take advantage of the natural incline of the Seine river basin from the south-east to the north-west: the slope of 3 centimetres per metre was enough to enable sand to be swept along and sewermen to walk without slipping. The ovoid shape of the sewers facilitated flushing.

The Chirac-as-mayor regime developed the public spectacle of urban cleansing above ground, undermining that below. Donald Reid (*Paris Sewers and Sewermen*) describes the dual appeal of the forces for cleanliness on the surface of the city: street cleaners dressed in bright, fashionable, ecology-signifying green jumpsuits satisfy the traditionalists, who can watch the workforce sweep the streets with the famous (now plastic) twig brooms, while the youth can identify with the green knights with their vacuum-equipped motorbikes, on the lookout for dog shit. The sewermen have been reduced, through rationalisation and cost-cutting, from soldiers of hygiene to mere labourers. New forms of management, maintenance and cleaning have led to their demythification. A massive five-year renovation programme was begun in 1991.

A small section of this labyrinth (not far from the Eiffel Tower) has been equipped for public viewing. An exhibition of documents on the history of the sewers, followed by an audio-visual display about the workings of the system, maps eras as far back as Lutèce, the Middle Ages, the Renaissance, Napoléon 1, Paris in 1914 and Paris in the 1960s, when concern was raised about the sewers' intestinal suitability as conduits for

Eugène Belgrand, restored 1991–96

Eugène Belgrand, restored 1991–96

terrorist attacks. At every period the subterranean architecture irrigating the city has reflected political, economic and cultural battles in the development of health and hygiene within Parisian society above.

The underground journey is so extraordinary that everyone should experience it. A guided tour takes visitors through dripping tunnels, past waste-collection pits and along the edge of a murky grey river. Instructive but smelly.

Ian Nairn described a sewer-tunnel trip in 1968: 'This short journey along one of them is best described as an *opéra noir*: a big open boat in a dark tunnel smelling faintly of gas and piss, chain-driven by two massive *égoûtiers*. Your own personal *voyage à l'enfer*, shocked into a crazy normality by street names appearing at appropriate intervals. The weirdest sensation of all is the thud of the pneumatic post, a 19th-century invention which provides a better intra-city service than anything the 20th century can think up. The guide maintains a rational commentary from start to finish, which is probably just as well.'

ADDRESS entrance at the corner of quai d'Orsay and place de la Résistance, 7e
CLIENT Ville de Paris
METRO Alma Marceau
ACCESS open 11.00–17.00, last admission 16.00 winter, 17.00 summer. Closed Thursday, Friday and last three weeks of January. FF24

Eugène Belgrand, restored 1991–96

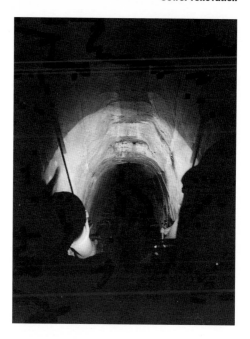

Quartier Latin to Opéra

Eugène Belgrand, restored 1991–96

Gare de l'Est to Bastille

Abribus

J C Decaux made his first million with a bus stop. His ingenious idea, in the 1950s, was to supply and maintain bus stops for local authorities. In return he earned the right to let advertising space on them. Reputedly the third richest man in France, he can now subcontract to Sir Norman Foster. The Foster bus stop, a 'bus-shelter system', is neat, normal and grey and can be spotted dotted along the Champs-Elysées.

Gare de l'Est to Bastille

ADDRESS all over Paris, for example on the Champs-Elysées, 8e
CLIENT J C Decaux
METRO Champs-Elysées
ACCESS open

Sir Norman Foster and Partners 1994

Gare de l'Est to Bastille

Sir Norman Foster and Partners 1994

Métro: Ligne Météor

The Paris métro (Métropolitan) is under the auspices of RATP (Régie Auto-nome des Transports Parisiens – brilliant logo on tickets), the parent organisation that oversees the métro and bus systems. The RER (super-subway) is independent, as is the SNCF (national rail network). Paris, 40 years behind London in starting an underground rail system, has under-stood that public transport is an infallible index to the health of a modern city and as a result is now a world leader in transport planning.

That RATP made its new Météor line the subject of an architectural competition, launched in 1990, seemed an enlightened idea, though the implementation of Köhn's winning design has proved problematic. Köhn and his team proposed a global strategy for the line, with the use of lightwells introducing natural light to quash the insalubrious image of travellers being led blindly down interminable corridors. The potential clearly exists to create a system where the traveller is not only oriented, but understands how the lines are organised relative to his or her journey. The success of the scheme depends on the lighting, the articulation of volumes and the materials used. A 25-metre life-size model has been built in a warehouse to test these criteria – an alternative to architects' coded drawings.

Köhn's intention was to establish an approach that would unify the renovation of six stations: Porte de Clichy, Place Clichy, St-Lazare, Madeleine, Pyramides and Bercy. However, the core of his design – a large vertical lightwell – has gradually been eroded by codes, regulations and demoralising bureaucracy. Almost extinct, it exists as a shrunken version at Madeleine only.

That the intelligence of Köhn's proposals could be so readily disre-garded by RATP shows a dearth of enlightened leadership. Comparable organisations such as the SNCF and the French post office have achieved

Gare de l'Est to Bastille

Bernard Köhn 1994–

Gare de l'Est to Bastille

Bernard Köhn 1994–

supportive and imaginative collaborations with architects that have made financial sense while projecting an image of French intellectual creativity well beyond its shores.

The inauguration of the first phase of Ligne Météor will unveil a métro shooting towards the twenty-first century. Fully automated and driverless, the train will operate like a horizontal elevator. A continuous wall of doors will align with a similarly doored wall at each station.

Changes at street level will be less evident. Long escalators slip in progressive tiers into the underground world of Paris, carrying with them a little of the urban life from above in the form of various services provided at intermediate landings. Köhn suggests that 1 per cent of RATP profit should be allocated to support temporary exhibitions of contemporary art. Meanwhile Sandrine, the giant tunnelling machine, grinds on.

Gare de l'Est to Bastille

ADDRESS Station Madeleine, 8e
CLIENT RATP
METRO Madeleine
ACCESS none yet

Bernard Köhn 1994–

Gare de l'Est to Bastille

Bernard Köhn 1994–

Opéra Garnier renovation

J'*assiste* à une pièce.
Peter Brook, *The Empty Space*

On the way to the opera in 1858 Napoléon III was almost assassinated in an explosion that killed 150 Parisians and the two horses pulling his carriage. This near miss caused him to replan the *quartier*, demolishing the narrow winding streets which had harboured the ambushers, creating a new avenue and commissioning a new opera house, through a competition, in 1861. The 36-year-old architect Charles Garnier was subject to the usual economic problems – his budget was cut from FF29 to 18 million, then again to 15 million. Garnier was so incensed, and expressed his feelings so strongly, that the budget was restored to FF21 million. Thirteen years and 30,000 drawings later, after excavations that had drained all the wells of the neighbourhood, the Opéra Garnier was completed.

Described with architectural acuity by Ian Nairn as 'a declamatory *roulade* of allegory ... more operatic than opera', the waiting space of this building is a sumptuous stage set for self-display. The performance itself was an intermission between the overtures, grand marches, love duets and choruses being played out by the *grands bourgeois* in the vestibules, galleries, anterooms and on the gorgeous sequence of double staircases leading to the mere auditorium (seating 2000).

Under the architectural direction of Roubert, Paris-based *scénographe* Scène, assisted by London-based engineers Ove Arup & Partners, are renovating the flytower – an 'empty space', strangely orthogonal in this voluptuous musical box. The main renovation is of the scenery hangers which operate in string-puppet fashion. Modern set-changes are increasingly generated from around the stage or below, where hydraulic arms telescope scenery into position. The stage platform may also spin sections

Gare de l'Est to Bastille

Jean-Loup Roubert (museum) 1992

Jean-Loup Roubert (museum) 1992

backstage, if such space exists. But in city sites, where the footprint is likely to be constrained by adjacent buildings, set change usually has to work vertically, the horizontal plane being taken up by the audience at the front, costume space for performers at the sides, and delivery access at the back. The age-old custom of hanging painted cloth has remained largely unchanged, affording as it does numerous economies: cheapness of materials, lightness which allows a basic counterweighted pulley system (like a giant sash window) to be easily manipulated by people and the cloth compactly rolled up for storage. Sophisticated computerised sequencing orchestrates effects: light, sound and set. Standing on the stage of the Opéra Garnier, one is awed under a 30-metre towering void.

One of the wings of the Opéra has also been renovated to create a library-museum. The Opéra's archives include an extensive collection of models and engravings now hung on glass walls designed by Roubert. New practice rooms for the dancers have been provided under the front cupola, while the lecture hall boasts wild-cherrywood furniture created by the *scénographe* Richard Peduzzi. (A *scénographe* is essentially an architect who specialises in theatre, set design, lighting and related technical aspects. There is no equivalent in Anglo-Saxon countries.)

ADDRESS Opéra Garnier, 8 rue Scribe, 9e
CLIENT Ministère de la Culture/Direction du Patrimoine/Direction de la Musique et de la Danse/Fondation Louis Vuitton/SNT
SCENOGRAPHIE library-museum, Richard Peduzzi; flytower, Scène
CONTRACT VALUE FF63 million (flytower)
METRO Opéra/Chaussée d'Antin
ACCESS museum open every day 10.00–16.30, FF30

Jean-Loup Roubert (museum) 1992

Jean-Loup Roubert (museum) 1992

Passage Brady renovation

Passage Brady (1828) was wrecked about half a century ago when the creation of the broad, heavy-duty traffic conduit, boulevard de Strasbourg, chopped this delicate glassy pedestrian alleyway in two. Erasing half the shops and more than a century of accretive culture, the new boulevard destroyed the ecology of the communities whose daily lives used to weave through this lively covered street. A second lease of life for passage Brady has been granted by the appointment of Lemoine as architect in charge of its renovation. Lemoine is well known for his historical research and writing on the architectural heritage and plight of the *passages* of Paris, many of which have fallen into disrepair and teeter on the threshold of dereliction and extinction.

Classic *passages* to visit in the second *arrondissement* include passage du Grand-Cerf between 145 rue St-Denis and 8 rue Dussoubs (1824); and passage du Bourg-l'Abbé between 120 rue St-Denis and 3 rue de Palestro, by Lusson (1828). Here the two *passages* form a continuous glass-vaulted slip route. Passage Choiseul, 40 rue des Petits-Champs and 23 rue Saint-Augustin, by Mazois and Tavernier (1825), has a simple hovering glass awning protecting the Ionic columns and arches that march between a maverick *melée* of seventeenth-century façades, nineteenth-century skylight construction and late-twentieth-century wares. The passage des Panoramas at 11 boulevard Montmartre and 10 rue St-Marc by Victor Grissart (1800, modified 1834) is composed of confident neo-classical columns and arches above which the spidery black ironwork supports glazing. The most wonderful improvisational glass tailoring can be strolled under in passage du Caire, 2 place du Caire. Constructed in 1799, this is a whole slice of city under glass, with cross-avenues, side turnings and half a dozen separate exits.

The project for passage Brady will entail a great deal of work, including

Bertrand Lemoine 1992–

Bertrand Lemoine 1992–

the remaking of centipedal stretches of the glass roof. But most difficult will be the territorial negotiations with the shop-owning residents to disentangle and, if necessary, redistribute the occupation of the grotto-like shop spaces in order to restore the architecture. Over time the shop bays have dissolved as a result of entrepreneurial initiatives: cosmetic shopfront modifications and extensions have concealed and destroyed the regular column rhythm and the façades of the original architecture. Only three bays out of 50 remain intact.

After years of neglect, orphaned by the city, passage Brady promises to respond well to this overdue love, care and attention. However, one can only hope that the zeal which inspires its resurrection is tempered by an affection for its evolved imperfections. That it does not become so sparkling new that the scents and eccentricities of its present-day cultures are sanitised under an uncomfortable shine.

Gare de l'Est to Bastille

ADDRESS 33 boulevard de Strasbourg, 10e
CLIENT Ville de Paris/DAU/private investors
METRO Strasbourg-St-Denis/Château d'Eau
ACCESS open

Bertrand Lemoine 1992–

Bertrand Lemoine 1992–

TGV – Eurostar

… nothing since the Eiffel Tower has captured the public imagination quite so strongly as the Trains à Grande Vitesse.
Frances Anderton and F A Pater, *Architectural Review*, May 1989

Centralised infrastructure planning has been integral to the development of France since the reign of Louis XIV. The TGV Atlantique project has involved the construction of eight new stations and the reconstruction of 20 others. 'Chief SNCF architect Jean-Marie Duthilleul's new stations and the livery and interiors of Roger Tallon's trains appear to combine very French characteristics: a love of engineering, of speed and of the sea – unifying colours of silver, blue and grey, a corporate image of speed and optimism. The essence of the design is a visual accord between building and train.'

Before take-off, the Eurostars trail alongside the 400-metre platforms like snakes with poisonous markings, aerodynamic snouts well into the commercial trough of the concourse. Inside the carriages the feeling is of a brand-new liner-cum-hotel: lots of flap-down, flip-up 'rests' for food and feet, a bar that encourages leaning and serves *espresso*, train-to-shore telephones and handle-free bathrooms that are a tap-dance of foot-pedal controls. Stepping on in central London and stepping off three hours later in central Paris is the closest we've come to time travel.

ADDRESS Gare du Nord, 10e
CLIENT BR/SNCF/SNCB
LENGTH 393.720 metres; POWER 12,240 kW = 20 Formula 1 racing cars
COST £24 million per trainset (1988)
METRO Gare du Nord
ACCESS Eurostar with ticket only; other TGVs open access

Jones Jarrard, ADSA, INOV 1994–

Jones Jarrard, ADSA, INOV 1994–

Sports complex

The narrow city-block site is hemmed into the back streets of Bastille, surrounded by the densely packed apartments of a poor neighbourhood. Continuing their enlightened track record of appointing interesting, often young, often foreign architects to mixed-finance projects, the RIVP nominated the Italian Massimiliano Fuksas to provide a mixture of public amenities: housing, sports facilities and parking.

There is no single vantage point from which to view the project as a whole. Instead, it is fragmented into a series of responses to its boundary streets, each with a different character, breaking the complex down into a manageable size and scale with a distinctive graphic flair.

The mastery of this building lies in its section. The problem of integrating the large concrete volumes – sports hall and carpark – has been solved by sinking them into the ground. The roofs are used as external sports surfaces, the wire-mesh fence leaning out into the *quartier*, dissolving the building's edge into the street and drawing on an urban language of tough backyard ball games. The swooping section culminates in zinc-clad apartments.

Gare de l'Est to Bastille

ADDRESS 11 rue Candie, 11e
CLIENT Direction de la Jeunesse et des Sports
CONTRACT VALUE FF53 million
ACCESS exterior only

Massimiliano Fuksas 1992–93

Massimiliano Fuksas 1992–93

Rue Oberkampf housing and post office

Like the architecture of Christian de Portzamparc, in whose office he served his apprenticeship, Borel's work is highly figurative. He aims to re-inject enthusiasm and emotional colour, materiality and a passion for craftsmanship into the built environment, so that architecture becomes once again a sensual experience.

This building – a post office and housing for post-office employees – is one of several enlightened collaborations between the French post office and young architects (see Bourdeau, page 278). Behind the façade, a garden is carved into this habitable sculpture, the block site hollowed out from within the surrounding fabric. Borel has created a similar coutyard solution for his nearby RIVP housing project (1989) at 100 boulevard de Belleville, 19e.

The post office is at street level, accessed by a short bridge wide enough for only one person at a time to cross. The forecourt to the post office is an open-air balcony that looks down into a courtyard garden faced on two sides by apartments and open at the back beneath the surveillance of two futuristic object-figure towers. Above the post office foyer a demi-ellipse is cut out, floor through floor, penetrating upwards to the sky – a space that is the negative volume of the inhabited towers at the other end of the garden. Each part of the building is riddled with passageways – a characteristic of this *quartier*.

The dwellings exhibit a maximum of diversity, eschewing the one- or two-bedroom apartment norm. Here Borel has created a kaleidoscopic composition of familiar living patterns cut up and restitched to allow new stories to unfold. Solids emerge from voids, scales and densities gather and disperse, views fade, cut and are recalled through the use of changing natural light and route. There is a guarded use of colour on the internal

Gare de l'Est to Bastille

Frédéric Borel 1993

Frédéric Borel 1993

courtyard elevations: monochromatic greys, mute and matt, with a twist
of terracotta orange.

Borel must have engaged in nail-biting acrobatics with the building
regulations to achieve such plasticity of expression. And one marvels at
his budget juggling. The project feels very new and well detailed. Three
gardeners and cleaners were in evidence the day I visited, which bodes
well for the building's life-expectancy.

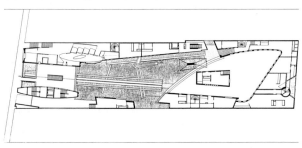

ADDRESS 113 rue Oberkampf, 11e
CLIENT Ministère des Postes et des Télécommunications/Toit et Joie
CONTRACTOR SGCPM
LANDSCAPING SNAE
SIZE 80 rented apartments, post office
METRO St-Maur
ACCESS exterior and view into courtyard only

Frédéric Borel 1993

Frédéric Borel 1993

Street markets

Temporary contemporary architecture is epitomised by the street market, a living, changing landscape of social and physical structures. The stalls' rusting steel ribcages are regularly reclothed in strut-stiffened fabric. Punters linger, queue and move on, fading away as the traders pack up the walls, fold up the roofs and take their leave.

The oldest market in Paris is Le Palu, set up near the Petit-Pont in the eleventh century. In 1136 Louis VI chose the area of Les Champeaux in the centre of Paris to open a new market which became Les Halles de Paris, a Crystal Palace of glass and cast-iron engineering designed by Victor Baltard, tragically demolished when the wholesalers moved out to suburban Rungis, near Orly airport, in 1973. In the fourteenth century shops proliferated to the detriment of markets, while the Hundred Years War interrupted trade. Les Halles revived somewhat in the sixteenth century, until Voltaire's disparaging comments of 1749 describing the markets as 'dirty, infection scattering and fermenting of disorder'.

Following the revolution, the Constituent Assembly reorganised the administration and addressed such criticisms by building covered markets on rue du Temple and St Honoré (now relegated to a parking lot). By 1824 there were 27 general markets in Paris, nine of them covered. This approach was consistent with the restructuring and decentralisation of the food trade and suppression of royal privilege which had historically monopolised market creation and ownership. From 1920 to 1938 the number of markets increased, especially on the outer boulevards along the line of the old city-wall fortifications, where they grew up at the same time as the HBM (low-rent housing projects).

Today Paris has more than 80 markets, open air, covered and specialist. Sited at crossroads, *places* and squares, prime trading positions are virtually hereditary. A fragile nomadic architecture, the markets' only protec-

Gare de l'Est to Bastille

tion is the energy and humour of the traders and customers.

To be comprehensively guided, refer to Nadia Pret's *Guide des Marchés à Paris*. For a less exhaustive taster, here are four market landscapes:

MARCHE DE BELLEVILLE relaxed, cosmopolitan, with herbs of all kinds, quantities of inexpensive shoes and exotic middle-eastern sweetmeats
ADDRESS boulevard de Belleville, from Faubourg de Temple, 11e
METRO Belleville
ACCESS open on Tuesday and Friday, 7.00–13.00

MARCHE DE LA BASTILLE a city dweller's idea of a country market in the middle of a high-speed boulevard
ADDRESS boulevard Richard-Lenoir, between place de la Bastille and rue St-Sabin, 11e
METRO Bastille/Bréguet-Sabin
ACCESS open on Thursday and Sunday, 7.00–13.00

MARCHE D'ALIGRE offers ground nuts and white rum for African dishes. A meeting place for militants who hand out pamphlets
ADDRESS rue and place d'Aligre, 12e
METRO Ledru-Rollin
ACCESS open Tuesday to Saturday, Sunday morning

MARCHE DE DAUMESNIL three artisanal pastry shops, one of which makes *chouquettes*, and a spice merchant. Fridays for fishmongers
ADDRESS place Félix-Eboué, boulevard Reuilly, to rue Charenton, 12e
METRO Daumesnil/Michel-Bizot
ACCESS open on Tuesday and Friday, 7.00–13.00

Tree gratings

Circular cast-iron tree gratings are one of the most evocative components of Parisian streets. The classic star-burst slots follow a nineteenth-century design by Adolphe Alphand and belong to a family of street furniture that includes lamp-posts, railings and benches.

The traditional version of the tree grating fulfils its function in a simple and adaptable way. The template can be modified to fit the varying widths of the tree trunks. Cast in four segments, of 45–50 centimetres in length, with a variable collar diameter of 60–100 centimetres, its configuration allows for the dismantling and replacing necessary to accommodate the growth of the trunk and the resurfacing of the street. The only problem is that the circular plan form requires paving stones to be cut to fit.

The Canal St-Martin was covered in 1860 by Belgrand (of the *égouts*, see page 92) and became a sewer, with the boulevard Richard-Lenoir riding atop. The renovation of the boulevard by the Mangin-Seura/Osty team has taken the idea of mapping the presence of the waterway concealed below through lighting, planting, paths and fountains.

The number of trees on the boulevard has justified the design of a new tree grating with a square frame. The new design captures the filigree patterns of moon-through-branches shadows, the joints dissolved by their jagged intersections and perfectly suited to casting.

ADDRESS boulevard Richard-Lenoir, 11e
CLIENT Ville de Paris/Direction des Parcs, des Jardins et des Espaces Verts
LANDSCAPE ARCHITECT Jacqueline Osty
METRO Bastille/Richard-Lenoir
ACCESS open

David Mangin-Seura, Jacqueline Osty 1995

David Mangin-Seura, Jacqueline Osty 1995

12ème arrondissement

Opéra de la Bastille

The Opéra de la Bastille holds a particularly important position at the intersection of key city-structuring routes. Towards the north-west, an axial cut leads through the six-storey nineteenth-century fabric of Paris, from the Colonne de Juillet in the place de la Bastille, through the Louvre, Grande Pyramide, Arche du Carrousel, the obelisk of place de la Concorde, up the Champs-Elysées to the Arc de Triomphe and out to La Défense with von Spreckelson's arch on the horizon. The second route leads north-east from the Arsenal waterway adjoining place de la Bastille, following the straightened curves of the buried canal under boulevard Richard-Lenoir, which re-emerges at place Stalingrad as the bassin de la Villette, and continues to become the Canal de l'Ourcq, running on through the Parc de la Villette to the suburbs. To the south-east the superb Viaduc Daumesnil stretches a line of 71 brick arches towards Bercy.

In the first flush of socialist triumph when Mitterrand was elected to the presidency in 1981, he proclaimed that there should be a popular opera house. Accessible to everyone, it would counter the image of opera as an elitist and expensive experience engendered by the blushing opulence of Garnier's royal masterpiece (see page 104). Popular meant with-it and lots of it: 24 operas a year were to be served up, mass culture for the masses.

Given the promised speed of delivery, elaborate backstage provision had to be made to facilitate the interchange between opera sets. As a result the theatre boasts seven complete stages around a turntable in addition to the main stage facing the auditorium. Scenery can be wheeled into position in minutes, while the whole arrangement is duplicated in cavernous cellars so that another battery of sets can be jacked up almost as quickly. This huge volume of storage determined the nature of the building.

Carlos Ott 1989

12ème arrondissement

Carlos Ott 1989

The Opéra site is a rough triangle, the blunt apex of which touches place de la Bastille. Disappointingly few of the competition designs attempted to reorganise the *place*, Ott's not at all. The stage complex had to go at the wide base of the triangle and the entrance had to be from the place de la Bastille itself for symbolic as much as functional reasons. The *place* is a large, loosely defined circus at the edge of the old city. The prison which was stormed on 14 July 1789 was a little to the west and the column in the *place*'s centre is a memorial to the fallen in the revolution of 1830. The *place* has always had symbolic importance for the French left so it was vital that the entrance to the people's opera should be from the people's *place*. The foyer and auditorium had to fit into whatever space was left. The elbow end is offset by a giant black granite portico which is inversely curved to accentuate the curve of the *place*.

The stepped white cladding follows the upward movement of the stairs which link all levels to the main entrance. These opaque panels combine with the opaque balcony balustrades to obscure much of the view of the *place* from within, while milling spaces cater meanly for the mob. That the life of the Opéra audience cannot be seen from the *place* and *vice versa* is a sadly missed opportunity.

If the anecdote is true – that the competition jury selected Ott's entry in the mistaken belief that it was by Richard Meier – then the jury members themselves are at least equally responsible for the mediocrity of the result. Another coincidence should be pointed out: the poor detailing of Ott's Opéra is shared by Gehry's American Center (see page 154). Both architects, foreign to Paris, were affiliated with the same local associate architects.

This building lacks human scale and contributes little to the experience of opera beyond the technical. The auditorium (with reputedly excellent

Carlos Ott 1989

Carlos Ott 1989

acoustics) is unglamorous, a spatially manipulable tool with no frills except for strips of boxes collaged on to the walls. To quote Peter Davey (*Architectural Review,* August 1989): 'How very different these spartan structures are from the boxes in Garnier's building which are very deep indeed, and cranked, with a couch in the back portion which cannot be seen from across the auditorium; in them, the pleasures of the performance and those of intimate companionship can be enjoyed separately or together.'

12ème arrondissement

ADDRESS place de la Bastille, 12e
CLIENT Ministère de la Culture et de la Communication/Etablissement Public de l'Opéra Bastille
ASSOCIATED ARCHITECT Saubot et Jullien
SIZE 2700-seat auditorium
METRO Bastille
ACCESS open

Carlos Ott 1989

Carlos Ott 1989

St-Antoine hospital kitchens

Like many others, the St-Antoine hospital was built in increments over a period spanning a century. The site of the kitchen addition is a residual lot on the north side of rue Citeaux, facing a T junction and inheriting a responsibility to address and close the view. On one side is a building of typical Parisian street scale, five storeys high. On the other is a two-storey neo-classical building to which a squat third storey has been added. Ciriani's task was that of urban infill: to darn the punctured plane of the street façade by mediating between these two buildings.

The plot is approximately 30 metres square, with all access from the rear via the hospital grounds. Without the need for street access, Ciriani was able to take the opportunity to explore the formal issues of the façade, a notoriously recalcitrant architectural problem.

The dogma of modernist space is that it is unbounded: it flows. Ciriani observed that seminal heroic schemes sacrificially anchor one corner of the plan (usually the services zone) in order to liberate the rest of the space. Haig Beck (*UIA*, issue 1, 1983) describes the *parti* of the St-Antoine kitchen, which follows this tenet, in terms of 'the servant (storage, preparation, cooking) and the served (distribution point)'. The services form a wall that limits two sides of the free-plan area containing the served space, which opens out on the diagonal towards the sun, embodying the modern heroic ethos of the hygienic, the rational and the efficient.

Pedestrians are routed round the loading bays before their path threads through the kitchen, weaving the hospital grounds into the addition. To marry the buildings on either side of the façade, a change in scale has been worked with the volumes around a roof garden. This capitalises on the orientation of the building and defines the way it reads from the street. With the sun always behind, the building is a silhouette, a delicate frame rather than a solid volume.

Henri Ciriani 1985

12ème arrondissement

Henri Ciriani 1985

Ciriani inventively uses the air-extraction plant to attain the various heights he needs. Air extractors are located over the open area of the plan. However, the ducts must be vented against the highest neighbouring building which required taking the exhaust pipe right across the façade to the plant tower at the corner. Thus the necessary 'volume' is achieved by using the route of the pipe as a frame. Meanwhile, the street is not denied sunshine.

For Ciriani sunlight is a vital and ideological component. His requirement that the sun should reach into the building suggested a series of rooflights on the garden terraces. As the building steps up, the sun penetrates at various levels; at the top of the building it pours through into the street.

Further ideological manipulations of the programme have influenced the volumetric resolution. From the initial requirements of the brief – changing rooms and a lounge – Ciriani has conjured a club for all the hospital ancillary staff. The volumes of the workers' club and the related roof gardens and loggia give the building its architectural content, superseding the function of the working area of the kitchen.

The blatantly Corbusian vocabulary is more than hagiography. The layered planes, simple rectangular openings, slip-form concrete curves and the *piloti* grid supporting the roof garden are the rational result of the manipulation of construction practices for pragmatic reasons. Programmatic and volumetric solutions are worked simultaneously.

ADDRESS 30 rue Citeaux, 12e
CLIENT Assistance Publique/Hôpitaux de Paris
METRO Faidherbe-Chaligny
ACCESS none

12ème arrondissement

Henri Ciriani 1985

Henri Ciriani 1985

Viaduc Daumesnil

In 1859 the new railway line Bastille–Bois de Vincennes, running west to east through the 12th *arrondissement*, was inaugurated. To avoid cutting up the district and to compensate for the uneven contours of the terrain, it was necessary to construct a viaduct. This calculated conduit follows in the noble-savage tradition of the functional French civil engineering which underpins the city of Paris (the sewers are another example, see page 92). The stocky city-scale centipede spans the 1.4-kilometre distance between place de la Bastille and ZAC Reuilly with its 71 brick arches.

The railway was decommissioned in 1969 and eventually the SNCF sold it to the Ville de Paris. The package included the station building, the viaduct situated on avenue Daumesnil, its embankments up to the goods station at Reuilly and the railway route extending as far as the Bois de Vincennes. The station was demolished to make way for the Opéra de la Bastille (see page 128) but the viaduct that led to it, now a national monument, remains.

The city decided to reinhabit the viaduct. This has been an inspired and unprecedented initiative of great benefit to the local communities of artists increasingly driven from the area by high rents. Historically the district of Bastille has supported a range of arts-and-crafts workers in ateliers hidden within the neighbourhood's alleys and courtyards. Carpet weavers, glass blowers, cabinet makers, lacquer layerers, printers and metal workers have co-existed interdependently to furnish the furniture galleries and shops of nearby Faubourg St-Antoine.

Commissioned to restore the viaduct to its original form, Berger has cleared away all the chalk-masonry infill. Each arch was then made habitable, with a cellar, street-level workspace and mezzanine. Glazed-in front and back with translucent and transparent panels, the studios retain the

12ème arrondissement

Patrick Berger, final phase 1995

aspect of arches, since light continues to pass through them, describing the repeating structure.

Thoughtfully and imaginatively, the now-vacant aerial route has been transformed into a little-known linear garden. Nine metres above the street, it is reached by stairs and lifts set at intervals. Trees and shrubs soften this bridge in a planted promenade envisaged to extend 4.5 kilometres from place de la Bastille out to the Bois de Vincennes.

12ème arrondissement

ADDRESS avenue Daumesnil, between rue Moreau and rue de Rambouillet, 12e
CLIENT Ville de Paris
LANDSCAPE ARCHITECT Philippe Mathieux
DIRECTION DE L'AMENAGEMENT URBAIN SEMAEST
RENT studios for artists: FF800 per square metre per year, ground floor; x 0.5 basement; x 0.7 mezzanine (approximately FF110,000 rent per arch per year). Shops and exhibitions: FF1500–1800 per square metre per year, ground floor; x 0.5 basement; x 0.7 mezzanine (approximately FF210,000–FF250,000 rent per arch per year)
SIZE 71 arches/1.4 km: 56.5 renovated; seven for use by the city; 7.5 public passages 75 square metres (ground level); 75 square metres (basement); 30–60 square metres (mezzanine option)
METRO Bastille/Gare de Lyon/Daumesnil
ACCESS open

Patrick Berger, final phase 1995

Patrick Berger, final phase 1995

Ville de Paris offices

Since the development of the *hôtels particuliers* with their grand and guarded porches, Paris has been a city of coded entrances. Nowadays entry is usually controlled by the prosaic means of buzzers – electronic locking systems with secret door codes. Porte Monumentale, as it is known colloquially, is one of the more imaginative of the office infill developments found throughout Paris. Built at the intersection of curving road, river and elevated railway, the entire 28 x 36-metre wall is a sliding door.

The success of Zubléna's scheme lies in a single idea which solves a number of problems. The gigantic sliding door opens on to a small court-yard-atrium which houses a glamorous reception hall serving the unremarkable municipal offices above. Economically politic, the architect concentrates the budget on one extravagant and highly visible gesture.

At 9.00 the door rolls open at a slow walking speed with a guard marching in front to warn pedestrians as if it were an early motor car. As the building starts to overlap itself, an intriguing series of shifting grid overlays and changing reflections appears. The door takes five minutes to open, and closes at the end of the working day, at 18.00.

The Porte Monumentale glides open and closed seemingly unaided. All the visual clues to its movement have been obscured. The motors lie in the basement of the building, the wheels are hidden Cadillac-style behind the bodywork of the door, while the hollow circular sections of the steel elements are larger than structurally necessary in order to contain the circuits and batteries. The door recharges when it is replaced in its closed position.

The glazing is hung imbricately, like inverted fish scales. The top of each pane leans outwards while the bottom is nudged in. Each panel is fixed continuously on its vertical edges. The purpose of this configuration

Aymeric Zubléna 1992

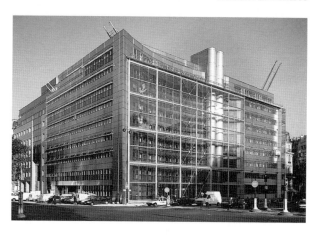

Aymeric Zubléna 1992

is to direct smoke out of the building in the event of a fire, while any water that penetrates this glass screen is guided back out using conventional curtain-wall detailing.

Porte Monumentale is a courteous continuation of the formal street front. While its architectural rhythms are as independent as its materials are a contrast to the soft patinas of its rendered and shuttered surroundings, there exists a Cageian concert of scales. The delicacy of good modern steel detailing responds to the decorative iron fronds of adjacent balustrades.

Best views riding métro lines M1 or M5.

12ème arrondissement

ADDRESS 94–96 quai de la Rapée, 12e
CLIENT Ville de Paris
CLIENT DELEGUE Délégués Généraux aux Affaires Sanitaires et Sociales, de l'Enfance et de la Santé
BET Séchaud et Bossuyt
STRUCTURAL ENGINEER RFR
CONTRACT VALUE FF142 million
SIZE 20,000 square metres
METRO Gare de Lyon/Bercy/Gare d'Austerlitz
ACCESS foyer only, unless on business

Aymeric Zubléna 1992

Aymeric Zubléna 1992

Ministère de l'Economie et des Finances

For some time the Louvre had needed to expand and had wanted to move the finance ministry out of the Richelieu Wing (see page 28). Thoughts of a new building for the tax collectors, mooted in General de Gaulle's era, eventually came to fruition following the Mitterrand directive to use the whole of the Louvre as a museum.

The national competition launched in 1982 for this complex at Bercy was for a 5-hectare strip already part-owned by the state, and chosen at the request of the city to boost plans for the regeneration of eastern Paris. Chemetov and Huidobro's vast wall/bridge structure defied the brief by striding over the rue de Bercy, the quai de Bercy expressway and contentiously clod-hopping into the Seine. The looming presence of this 'Palace for Tax Returns' – home to 6000 head-scratching debt collectors and switchboard *tricoteurs* – demands attention as unavoidably as the end of the financial year. Hiding a powerful chunk of government above the great two-storey marble-paved hall that runs the length of the four major bays, the glamour of this piece of state architecture is indistinguishable from the corporate glitz of private enterprise.

The edifice reads like a mega-version of the elevated section of the métro line that rises from cutting to viaduct on top of the Bercy bridge. Its court-punctuated configuration frames views through to the river. Black glazing gazes over Paris in dispassionate surveillance. The building was restricted to a height of 34 metres, 4 metres lower than the adjacent Palais Omnisports. Arm-twisting changes to floor areas and budget were surmounted, the idea of viaduct and vista strong enough to survive bureaucratic bastardisation.

The building forms a great stone-clad, precast polished-concrete and metal-trussed L. A similarly scaled slab running east–west is joined to the

Paul Chemetov, Borja Huidobro 1990

Paul Chemetov, Borja Huidobro 1990

Gare de Lyon by an upper-level, open-air pedestrian walkway. The ministry is an important urban structuring element, large enough to give a sense of scale to the Omnisports octagon and to offset the amorphous development anticipated on the left bank around the Bibliothèque de France (see page 172). Its role as a containing device is akin to that of a rampart running parallel to the dry-moat métro cutting which, together with a series of access bridges over green ditches, suggests a city wall.

Lying on the approximate line of the wall of the Fermiers Généraux of the 1780s, the ministry defines the boundary between Paris and the former suburbs. The huge portal suggests a gateway and is evocative of Ledoux's *barrières* – the toll-houses (of which the Barrière de La Villette in place de Stalingrad is a surviving example) built to control and tax all goods entering the capital. But the ministry does not halt the commuter traffic which drives through its inhospitable gateway.

Official residence of the minister of finance (arguably the third most powerful man in France), the two-storey polyscopic penthouse in the prow of the 'pier' overhangs the swirling Seine. It commands unassailable views through bullet-proof glass over central Paris and the ZAC de Bercy, and has back-door access to the get-away helipad and water-launch.

ADDRESS 139 rue de Bercy, 12e
CLIENT Ministère de l'Economie et des Finances
ARCHITECTS-CONSEIL Emile Duhart-Harosteguy
CONTRACT VALUE FF2930 million (1984)
SIZE 225,000 square metres
METRO Bercy/Quai de la Gare
ACCESS none

Paul Chemetov, Borja Huidobro 1990

12ème arrondissement

Paul Chemetov, Borja Huidobro 1990

Temporary American Center

All architecture is temporary. And though some buildings undoubtedly last a long time, few address ideas which could be described as timeless. Ironically, it is often types of enclosure designed to be temporary – such as market canopies, which existed in Teheran 2000 years ago in much the same form found in Paris today – that display an intelligent simplicity which allows their structure to survive for centuries virtually unchanged. And what we commonly understand as temporary buildings are often the underestimated forerunners of more permanent architecture, where ideas can be tested in ways unavailable to structures requiring longer-term commitment. Yet the improvised, the propped and the entropic are marginalised forms of spatial existence.

The Temporary American Center, forerunner to the (permanent) American Center (see page 154), follows in a tradition of spatially inventive exhibition enclosures. The site was, and is, the wedge-shaped island park or public 'square' between the ZACs of Bercy and Chalon. The short story of the project is of a park that briefly became a building, only to return to a park.

Given the story, the trees had to stay. As in most Parisian parks, these are arranged in straight rows on gravel. Seraji's project involved the trees as part of the architecture, symbols of temporality, change and movement, growth and protection. In plan, trees and columns are indistinguishable. In section or elevation, trunks and columns read blurrily through translucent 'windows' in the chipboard enclosure. The building uses straight but not parallel lines and planes, in which the trees speed up the rhythm and perspective, pocketed in exterior modules that form individual tree rooms under an open roof. The rhythm is carried into the city by a row of small nineteenth-century workers' houses.

So why was this fully functional building demolished? The building

Nasrine Seraji December 1991–February 1994

12ème arrondissement

12ème arrondissement

Nasrine Seraji December 1991–February 1994

was costing the American Center the rental of the square. A Parisian public square, by statute, belongs to the public and cannot be built upon. Planning permission had only allowed 24 to 36 months of occupancy. The Ville de Paris said the square was needed as a public space, but its ulterior motives were more complex.

Like most European cities, Paris has homeless people. Winter was approaching. The media had got hold of the idea that 130 people could be housed in this building, empty since the completion of Frank Gehry's American Center in May 1993. Because of the publicity there was an immediate problem with squatting. The government didn't want squatters or homeless people in such a prestige site, while the Ville de Paris was worried that if something designated temporary became permanent it would set a precedent: once occupied, the building could not easily be demolished and then the square would be lost for good. In February 1994 the bulldozers moved in with uncharacteristic municipal efficiency. Now all that remains are the trees and the gravel – and the frown of something half remembered.

12ème arrondissement

ADDRESS 51 rue de Bercy, 12e
CLIENT SCI American Center
BET Dupont Setec
BUREAU DE CONTROLE Socotec
DEMOLITION Marande et Fils
CONTRACT VALUE FF5 million
SIZE 906 square metres
METRO Bercy
ACCESS irrelevant

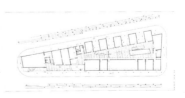

Nasrine Seraji December 1991–February 1994

12ème arrondissement

American CenterFrank Gehry is a Californian Stig of the Dump. Stig, in the classic children's book, is a Stone-Age inhabitant of a rubbish tip at the bottom of a garden who makes his home by an imaginative and inventive use of refuse. Gehry's own house, on the Santa Monica beach strip of Los Angeles, was described in the *New Yorker* (October 1994) as 'a post-cyclone accumulation of industrial debris'. Passers-by would be unlikely to call it beautiful. Unusual maybe, interesting perhaps, even ugly.

The American Center aims to promote understanding between the United States and France through social, educational and cultural activities available to the public. Looking for a site on which to expand, the organisation was lured from boulevard Raspail (now the Fondation Cartier, see page 184) and offered a persuasive package and prime location on the banks of the Seine. A new building, authored by Gehry, it was reasoned, would act as a perfect catalyst for the ZAC de Bercy, and would be guaranteed to attract attention, if not a few sparks.

Using an extraordinary version of the organisation of James Stirling's History Faculty Library in Cambridge, England, the building is a cascade held on two sides by blocks in the shape of an L. The road and alley façades display the unerring sobriety of traditional Parisian street fronts with ordinary window openings in regular lines on matter-of-fact vertical walls which then disintegrate extravagantly in a series of drunken lurches/earthquake slippages towards the south-west parkscape.

Our preconceptions about the weight of stone, in which the building is clad, are manipulated. Vertical mortar joints are stepped incrementally, giving the faint impression of diagonal ladders running up and down the façades. The unbuttoned side of the building, its contortions spelled out in stone, becomes a strangely establishment-permanent version of Gehry's casual-temporary wire-mesh and chipboard vocabulary.

Frank O Gehry and Associates, Inc. 1994

12ème arrondissement

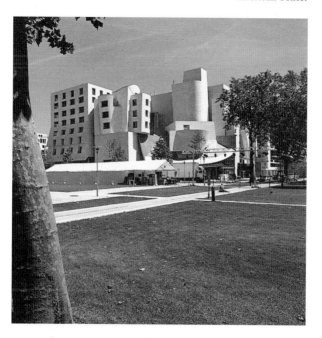

Frank O Gehry and Associates, Inc. 1994

On the north-west corner the yellowish limestone skin, quarried at St-Maximin (APUR instructions insisted on French stone), slants out to create two pelmets which, sharply angled in section, turn the wall into a zinc-covered rooftop shape – a familiar sight for the *chambre-de-bonne* – while approximating a *piano nobile* level, simply glazed, full height, within galvanised steel frames. On the south-east corner glass wings flap down the side of the building, allowing light to enter the gallery space behind: watch out for the dangerous blades of the curtain wall as it hits the ground. Optical and psychological experimentation resumes towards the park where strange clustered stone formations hover above and rest upon the big zinc-skirt-swathed entry (reminiscent of the elephant's tutu in *Fantasia*) in an uncomfortable inversion of structural sense.

The exterior forms are an adequate expression of the wonderful interior reception-gallery, a restful transition space overlooking the park and river. Lit by irregularly shaped skylights and traversed by walkways above, it is intruded into by mezzanine levels in such a way that it begins to resemble a light-filled mountain gorge.

The staircase is particularly successful, though it is rarely used. It connects the exhibition spaces to the upper lobby and looks on to an internal roof terrace, a vertical courtyard space serving the 26 apartments for visiting artists and scholars. The offices are banal. Disorienting, badly lit, totally internal corridors wind into an unnecessarily deep plan. The building did not have to be a block, and Gehry could have created many more light-penetrating and orienting voids than he has done.

The rue de Bercy wing provides a 400-seat theatre at an intimate scale, much like a theatre in a *château*. There is a 100-seat cinema and lecture hall, an art gallery with more than 10,000 square feet of exhibition space, two black-box spaces for performance and sound and film recording, an

Frank O Gehry and Associates, Inc. 1994

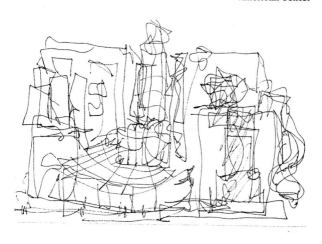

Frank O Gehry and Associates, Inc. 1994

audio-visual centre, executive offices and a subterranean parking garage, as well as spaces set aside for a bookstore and a design shop.

While the park façade is playful, it does nothing with space beyond a loud percussion of parts that shout 'entrance'. The building form has no obvious political value, its display alone justifying its existence. It seems a missed opportunity not to have sculpted the park as part of the conversation.

The building remains a fun object, an architectural soliloquy that neither up-ends the constraints of Parisian building codes nor turns them to advantage with the dextrous wit Gehry is famed for. One is puzzled, if not nettled, that the architect doesn't seem to care to engage with the culture of the city. The American Center is just not Gehry enough.

On 23 January 1996, less than three years after its completion, a decision was taken to sell the American Center. For further information call 44·73·77·77·

ADDRESS 51 rue de Bercy, 12e
CLIENT SCI American Center Bercy/SEMAEST
ASSOCIATED ARCHITECTS Saubot et Jullien
CLIENT REPRESENTATIVE Sinvim
BET/STRUCTURAL ENGINEER SGTE
BUREAU DE CONTROLE Socotec
CONTRACTOR Petit
CONTRACT VALUE FF158 million (1991)
SIZE 12,455 square metres
METRO Bercy
ACCESS open

12ème arrondissement

Frank O Gehry and Associates, Inc. 1994

12ème arrondissement

Frank O Gehry and Associates, Inc. 1994

Centre Commercial Bercy II

French cities retain their charm by relegating unalluring urban realities and traffic to the outskirts. Shedlands (a term coined by F A Pater), resulting from the migration of large commercial outlets to areas 'without' the city walls, have been the prime cause of the continued pleasantness of so many town centres. Single-storey corrugated metal, fibreglass and asbestos-cement buildings sprawl on potholed tracts of concrete or tarmac, with carparks invariably littered with the detritus of deliveries.

Bercy II is part of a ZAC created under the Charenton-le-Pont local authority on land previously occupied by wine warehouses. Designed to impress at the scale of the motorway and speed of the car, it is positioned in the no-man's land between the périphérique and the autoroute de l'Est.

Bercy II belongs to a family of buildings whose enclosing form is a response to an inhospitable environment created by a nearby traffic interchange, its entrance difficult to find by car and life-threatening by foot. By the time Piano was brought in, the building permit had been obtained, the structural grid fixed and the underground carpark specified: decisions taken on the basis of insufficient information which had to be lived with. The double-skin curved roof covering is carried on a steel and laminated-timber structure, a silk-purse solution designed to be supported by the inherited sow's-ear layout of concrete columns.

The cladding is a self-advertising element. In addition to the neon signs that adorn it, light from the traffic is reflected mutedly in its metal panels. The industrial language of its form is stiffly articulated in facets, more Tin Man from Oz than Spielbergian UFO. Softened against the greys of the Parisian horizon – zinc roofs and overcast sky – the outer skin is of stainless-steel 'tiles', perforated to let light in or smoke out. These panels also protect the vast curvilinear roof from sunlight and wind. Easily unclipped for maintenance, they are lapped the opposite way from slates

Renzo Piano Building Workshop 1990

12ème arrondissement

Renzo Piano Building Workshop 1990

to allow a certain amount of rain penetration to clean a second inner skin which provides waterproofing and insulation. The sculpted form is defined by three sectors of circles, each with a different radius. The fine difference between each of the curved surfaces is absorbed at the joints between the panels, which have a standard 30-centimetre width and are between 80 centimetres and 2 metres long.

The double skin mediates the different exterior and interior scales. From a strong outside statement of container surrounded by the chaos of a spaghetti junction, inside the clarity of the shell's supporting segments reigns over the whimsy of shopping-centre culture. It is difficult to appreciate the building's size from within. Organised around a long, oblong five-storey gallery, the interior has the clean, stripped air of an ocean liner. This is accentuated by the escalator ramps that span between bridges over the gallery space. The roof beams curve like a whale's ribcage, with porthole skylights and hatch-like ventilation openings punched through the inner skin but protected by the perforated steel panels of the outer skin. The garden with tall trees and a waterway was designed by Desvignes et Dalnoky (compare rue de Meaux apartments, page 256).

ADDRESS rue Escoffier, Charenton-le-Pont, Val-de-Marne
CLIENT GRC Emin
ARCHITECT RESPONSABLE Jean-François Blassel
CONSULTANT ENGINEER Ove Arup & Partners
LANDSCAPE ARCHITECT Desvignes et Dalnoky
SIZE 47,000 square metres parking; 1,100,000-square-metre shopping centre
METRO Liberté
ACCESS open

12ème arrondissement

Renzo Piano Building Workshop 1990

12ème arrondissement

Renzo Piano Building Workshop 1990

13ème–14ème arrondissements

Technical and administrative cité

On a nondescript strip of grassland in the peripheral city, where recent constructions rely on bulk for effect (with exceptions: see Perrault's *hôtel industriel*, page 168, and Piano's Bercy shopping centre across the Seine, page 160), a bifurcated slab towers over an extruded and perforated plinth. The parapet of the horizontal base, or wavy 'landscape' as Kagan calls it, is aligned with the surface of the périphérique. This softness and continuity emphasise the cut-out quality of the office slab against the sky, like an image in a pop-up book.

The users belong to two different bureaucracies. The bar butting on to the entrance gate is a garage for the *brigade d'intervention*, motorised patrollers of the périphérique. Beneath the undulating concrete roof are vehicle bays in which the maintenance crews who tend the public parks and fountains bivouac.

The observer is left uncertain as to whether the *cité* is one or many buildings.

13ème–14ème arrondissements

ADDRESS 5 quai d'Ivry, 2–4 rue Brunesseau, 13e
CLIENT Ville de Paris, RIVP
METRO Porte d'Ivry
RER Boulevard Masséna
ACCESS none

Michel Kagan 1991

Michel Kagan 1991

Hôtel Industriel

Perrault is interested in the idea of the disappearing surface – making nothing out of something – and the envelope of this *hôtel industriel* is as continuous and as virtual as its glass detailing will allow. The architect has tried to minimise the outward appearance of this volume until it resembles a vacuum-packed, shrink-wrapped shelving system, its concrete structure enveloped by a slick and efficient skin. The approach is two dimensional and the emphasis on surface image projects a sense of technological contemporaneity and sensuous minimalism.

The *hôtel industriel* sits on the edge of the périphérique among the off-ramps and railway lines feeding the Gare d'Austerlitz like a rectangular aquarium, glaucous green in colour. If this architecture is about planes and edges, it has much in common – not least proportionally – with the motorway billboards from which glamorous ladies offer 36 15 numbers for sexy telephone calls.

The project came about for protective reasons. For centuries cities were centres for craft activities and trades, with carpenters, locksmiths, cabinet-makers, wheelwrights and so on located in groups in certain districts, bringing life and character to the urban environment. But as a result of rent increases, factories and workshops have started to move to outlying wasteground and suburbs. To counter this migration from Paris, the mayor called for new *hôtels industriels* – a hybrid of warehouse, workshops and offices, 'neither an office building nor an industrial building, but simply an "intelligent" space' – to be built to retain such activities within the capital. Won in competition in 1986, Perrault's *hôtel industriel* houses about 40 small industrial concerns as well as the architect's own office.

On closer perusal the building reveals a wonderful transparency, especially at its corners, where services are expressed, if in a less aggressive

Dominique Perrault 1990

Dominique Perrault 1990

fashion than at the Centre Pompidou (see page 66). The thin horizontal lines of floors and tubular silver air-conditioning ducts set against the glass wall at ceiling and floor levels are both visible. Most intriguing are the six wafer lines created by the crude perforated-metal *brise-soleil* shelving that runs all the way around the building on each floor, dressed with files, various materials, or hard hats depending on the nature and business of the occupants. This horizontal emphasis is checked by the vertical mullion lines of the glass cladding panels. The building can be seen as a dramatic reversal of the traditional Parisian façade, its clear planar forms articulated by 'balconies' on the inside.

From inside, the spaces offer hypnotic views of the perpetual motion of Paris at least as distracting as the views of the Thames from Norman Foster's London office. This is one of the must-be-seen buildings in Paris, if only for its role as the harbinger of Perrault's massive monument for the nearby Bibliothèque de France (see page 172).

ADDRESS 26 rue Brunesseau, 13e
CLIENT SAGI
BET Technip
BUREAU DE CONTROLE Véritas
CONTRACT VALUE FF72 million (July 1987)
SIZE 15,000 square metres
METRO Porte d'Ivry/Quai de la Gare
RER Boulevard Masséna
ACCESS none

Dominique Perrault 1990

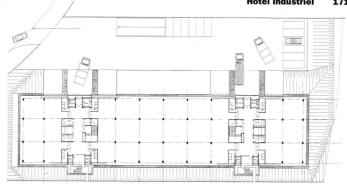

13ème–14ème arrondissements

Dominique Perrault 1990

Bibliothèque de France

Perrault won the competition for the huge new national library of France at the age of 34. But the brief was for more than a library. Perrault inherited the responsibility of creating a project capable of providing a focus for the ZAC Seine Rive Gauche and supplying an identity for an area with no landmark historical connections. Further west, the left bank of the Seine has since the Middle Ages been the student district. This offered an opportunity for the library to link in with long-established educational programmes. Perrault's urban plan proposed an empty space, a quiet spot away from the fuss of the city. This place was aligned with the sequence of large empty spaces along the Seine: place de la Concorde, the Champs de Mars, Les Invalides.

The basis of Perrault's approach rests on the idea of creating a place, not a building. 'When I think library, I think first of all of a space for reading … It is more the place where one comes to read, rather than the place where there are books.' The main idea of the project is the virtual volume defined by the four corner towers (the analogy with open books is crude – Perrault should excise this impoverished one-liner). Within this he has planned a 2.5-hectare garden, the same size as the Palais-Royal. Gardens and learning have been inextricably linked since Genesis, not least in the architecture of Labrouste's main reading room within the old Bibliothèque Nationale (58 rue de Richelieu, 2e). Here filigree cast- and wrought-iron columns climb up into a canopy of nine ornate and hovering domes where light washes down the faïence flutes to mingle with readers' aspirations. However Perrault's garden is an untouchable Eden from which researchers and members of the public are barred.

A former head of the Bibliothèque Nationale, Georges Le Rider, presented Mitterrand with a petition signed by 700 intellectuals worldwide who unanimously agreed, for numerous common-sense reasons,

13ème–14ème arrondissements

Dominique Perrault 1995

Dominique Perrault 1995

that the project was 'spectacularly bad'. Rare books were to be stored in the 25 floors of the four glass towers, with the most frequently consulted books near the reading rooms below. This arrangement placed the most fragile books in the areas where they would be most vulnerable to light (although giving them a spectacular city view). Readers, on the other hand, were effectively underground, looking into the tonsorial topiary of the garden.

A report was authorised 'to defuse a situation of conflict that was in large part artificial', and a five-man commission named. The report is a masterpiece of tactfully phrased alarm, centring on environmental conditions and problems of organisation resulting from the building form. It was pointed out that on sunny days the temperature between the two outer layers of glass might reach 60 degrees Celsius.

Building work continued. Bouygues, the main contractor, was making record pours of concrete (2000 cubic metres per day), completing a floor every four days. Meanwhile Perrault launched an appeal for 'Mobilisation in favour of the French National Library Project', saying it would be 'disastrous for architecture to serve as an alibi for personal vendettas or as a backdrop for disputes among specialists'. The combination of Mitterrand's obstinacy, Perrault's refusal to alter his design, bureaucratically delayed reports and the speed of construction ensured that the project rapidly became too advanced for its opponents to kill it off.

Little has actually changed. The towers have been lowered by two storeys and fragile books are to be stored around the exterior of the reading rooms below. This has resulted in an ironic inversion: the more a book is read, the further it will be from the reader.

The transparency and immateriality of the towers has been undermined by the layers of sun-shading needed to protect the books. These

Dominique Perrault 1995

Dominique Perrault 1995

are now cocooned in an envelope made up of two outer layers of glass, a wooden sheath, rock wool insulation and a concrete shell. The most environmentally sensitive material will remain in the present Bibliothèque Nationale which will become the National Library for the Arts.

It is left to wood to provide this monument with warmth and life. The whole is framed as a temple with a huge, steep, stepped esplanade made of an indecent amount of rain-forest hardwood. Aesthetically the project offers nothing more as you move closer. The sketch diagram of four tower blocks at 1:10,000 does not develop any intriguing details at 1:1 – there is no depth to a minimal idea. The vastness of the space between the towers combined with their lack of surface variation leaves one with no place to anchor one's glance. The lack of relationship between the buildings leaves the space vacuous and forlorn.

The physical, financial, political and time constraints of the project have overwhelmed judgement. The strategy from the beginning appears to have been one of coping rather than mastering. When asked to comment, Perrault said: 'We just do it.'

ADDRESS 101 quai de la Gare, 13er
CLIENT Mission Interministérielle des Grands Travaux/Secrétariat d'Etat aux Grands Travaux/Etablissement Public de la Bibliothèque de France
AMENAGEUR SEMAPA
CONTRACT VALUE FF5.2 billion (1989)
SIZE 286,926 square metres
METRO Quai de la Gare
ACCESS open

Dominique Perrault 1995

13ème–14ème arrondissements

Dominique Perrault 1995

Grand Ecran

Paris is the city of cinema. The movie-palace classic is the Cinéma Rex, 1 boulevard Poissonnière, 2e, designed by John Eberson and André Bluysen in 1931. It is one of two great temples of cinema built in Paris between the wars, the other being the Gaumont Palace, which was pulled down in 1972.

As an institution of power and wealth, the cinema rivals the cathedral. The Grand Ecran, or Big [18-metre] Screen, poses as a monumental civic building on place d'Italie. It even has a spire.

Commissioned by Chirac, the Grand Ecran was Tange's first European building. One of eight enclosing blocks guarding the circular space of place d'Italie, this is a frontier zone rather than a gateway. Part of a reconstruction effort to heal the schism between the traditional Parisian fabric and 1960s tower blocks, the building scales down skilfully at the rue Bobillot junction with the Italie 2 shopping centre.

The monumental location and importance signified by the tower are compromised by the fact that the building merely houses offices for audio-visual production and projection, two cinemas, a hotel and a shopping mall. The glass screen under the squared arch of the place d'Italie façade gives access to cascading floor levels which lead to a blind wall rather than an important portal. The bow trusses which flex above this empty atrium (beneath which is located the huge cinema) are doubled within a blue glass wall.

It is a comment on this shiftiness of identity that the juxtaposed forms of the building focus on the glass tower which accommodates the lifts. Above this (to a height of 55 metres) extends a landmark sculpture by Thierry Vidé nicknamed 'the Campanile'. Engineer Sophie Le Bourva commented on the way Vidé's extension captures the vibrancy of a site under construction: 'a temporal period when the building is "alive"

Kenzo Tange and Associates 1991

Kenzo Tange and Associates 1991

before being gelled by completion, as seductive and woefully illusive as the architect's sketch model'.

The dynamically related collage of geometric pieces flying through space is intended to embody a metaphorical expression of cinema: communication, change, fading frames, transparencies. Some of the collection of suspended elements, 'arms' and 'cubes', were intended to move. Like a giant clock, the movements would have marked the times of the main events taking place inside the Grand Ecran. Despite the fact that all the necessary equipment is installed, the arms are not moving and the kinetic content of Vidé's work remains unknown to the public. However, movement is implicit if not actual: the sculpture changes as the sun and clouds animate it with light effects.

Check *Pariscope* or the *Officiel des Spectacles* for events.

ADDRESS 18–20 place d'Italie, 13e
CLIENT Societé Civile Immobilière Italie Grand Ecran
ASSOCIATE ARCHITECTS Xavier Menu, Michel Macary
SOCIETE GERANTE Foncière des Champs-Élysées promotion
CONSULTANT ENGINEER Ove Arup & Partners (Campanile)
SIZE 40,000 square metres
METRO Place d'Italie
ACCESS open

Kenzo Tange and Associates 1991

Kenzo Tange and Associates 1991

Stade Sébastien-Charléty

Stadia are civic monuments, landscape-sized buildings in which large audiences witness national events. Stadia in ancient Greece were race courses located between two hills which provided natural slopes for tiers of seating. This stadium is located in the band between the boulevard des Maréchaux and the périphérique in the *zone non aedificandi*, the apron of land left clear for cannon-fire from the last city wall (Thiers, 1841–45), the footprint of which lies under the boulevards.

Stade Charléty is read from the périphérique across the tapestry of the cemetery as an elliptical metal bowl curling over the contours. The palette is of greys: *chiaroscuro*, *grisaille*, oyster. Entry is on the west side, between the main part of the stadium and the National Olympic Committee building, which runs ship-like along avenue de la Porte-de-Gentilly. The space between these two main pieces is occupied by the lower structures of the lecture theatre and auditorium with their wave-like lead roofs. Between these structures a forecourt has been created – a mega milling space with a huge *escalier d'honneur* on which to linger before entering the auditorium of sport. The surface articulations, *piloti* and scale are incomparable with Le Corbusier's Brazilian Pavilion (1959) and Pavillon Suisse across the road in the Cité Universitaire campus.

ADDRESS avenue de la Porte-de-Gentilly, 13e
CLIENT Ville de Paris/Direction de la Jeunesse et des Sports/Direction de l'Architecture
BET/ENGINEER OTH Bâtiments
CONTRACTOR Bouygues
SIZE 20,000-seat stadium
METRO Place d'Italie/RER Cité Universitaire
ACCESS open

Henri and Bruno Gaudin 1994

Henri and Bruno Gaudin 1994

Fondation Cartier pour l'Art Contemporain

No. 261 boulevard Raspail, previously the American Center (see page 154), is the site where Chateaubriand (1768–1848, writer, statesman and precursor of the romantic movement in France) lived and planted a Lebanese cedar, which became a symbol of the left bank. This cedar (now 200 years into its probable 300-year life) is framed by two glass screens that form a gate, ensuring that visitors pass under its horizontal boughs on their way in to exhibitions.

The sheet-glass façades of the building extend beyond its structure, blurring its boundaries and denying the reading of a solid volume. On the top storey the façade extends for several metres above the level of the terrace, so the sky is read as a back projection. The trees acquire a similarly ambiguous presence as it is unclear whether they are inside or outside. The trees are read behind a transparent fence instead of an opaque wall, and are embodied in the building by means of the 8-metre-high sliding windows to the exhibition space which can be entirely removed in summer, undressing the structure to reveal the columns. This allows the exhibition to slide into the park and *vice versa*. The building is a refracting series of superimpositions of sky, trees and reflected trees. Nouvel and his team have tried to bottle the mystery that belongs to a secret, walled garden between these glass layers.

Light is filtered through screens behind the clear glass skin of the south and west façades. The material for these screens is a dense tulle of meshed steel. The escape staircases squeeze out from behind the building like outriggers, zig-zagging past the showcase offices. The lifts on the east façade are climbers – no cages, no wires – sliding up and down the glass façade. Superstructure echoes substructure as eight of the 16 levels are underground parking.

Jean Nouvel, Emanuel Cattani et Associés 1994

Jean Nouvel, Emanuel Cattani et Associés 1994

The antecedents of transparency as an architectural vogue in France lie in part in the Parisian fascination with modernity. Once material and constructional advances offered the possibility of see-through façades, architects such as Nouvel and Perrault immediately seized on this potential. The French love of film led to a poaching of visual devices from the editing room. Buildings could be 'animated', their ephemerality enhanced through perspectival layerings, sequential framing of views, fading light, superimpositions, reflections and entropic diurnal and seasonal changes (such as deliberate rusting). However, the reality of Nouvel's building remains a rather literal interpretation of such intentions.

Arguments for the merits of transparency were common in the 1960s. Yet the supposed democracy, or neutrality, of glass is ultimately frustrating, if not deceiving. While transparent, reflections permitting visual penetration sometimes, glass maintains a physical separation – you can see, but you can't have. Watch Jacques Tati's *Playtime*.

ADDRESS 261 boulevard Raspail, 14e
CLIENT GAN Vie
CLIENT DELEGUE COGEDIM
STRUCTURAL ENGINEER Ove Arup & Partners
LANDSCAPE ARCHITECT Ingénieur et Paysage
CONTRACT VALUE FF98 million
SIZE 6500 square metres of which 2500 square metres Fondation Cartier, 4000 square metres offices; gross floor area 11,300 square metres
METRO Raspail/Denfert-Rochereau
ACCESS open every day except Monday, 12.00–20.00 (Tuesday –22.00); FF20

13ème–14ème arrondissements

Jean Nouvel, Emanuel Cattani et Associés 1994

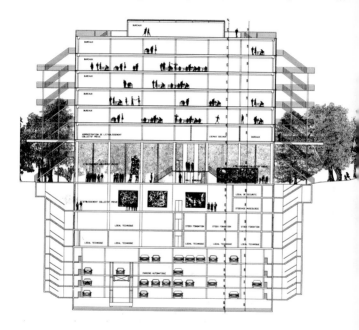

Jean Nouvel, Emanuel Cattani et Associés 1994

15ème arrondissement

Aquaboulevard de Paris

Fibreglass water slides writhe through the cathedral-high space, spewing swimmers into the Hawaiian blue, wave-machine surf and Jacuzzi massaging lagoons. Punters can lounge on sunchairs on the yellow terrazzo beach between craggy outcrops sprouting green trees and ferns approximating palms. Hot and steamy with chlorine, this plastic paradise is enormously popular. Its advertisement colours may be lurid, but they look fun. Climb into the time machine and leave the dreariness of winter for aquadise.

The organisational spine of the building is a mall of cafés, opticians, sports shops, record retailers, boutiques and a travel agent where starfish loll on blue satin in the window. From this commercial route the shopper can access interior sports facilities such as squash and tennis on one side while viewing fantasy island on the other. Future expansion includes indoor parks and a theatre.

Massive in scale, cheaply built and aesthetically indigestible, this extruded triangular tent clad in translucent corrugated plastic is framed by enormous glulam beams. Strange white panels hang down from the roof, presumably to baffle sound or diffuse light.

Cheerful and friendly, this leisure centre is accessed by car or via an inhospitable pedestrian route along main roads and under the périphérique. It is difficult to get a sense of the building from outside as it is sandwiched between a concrete tower and a heliport.

ADDRESS 4–6 rue Louis-Armand, 15e
CLIENT Société Nauticlub de Paris
METRO Balard
ACCESS open

15ème arrondissement

Alexandre Ghiulamila 1989

15ème arrondissement

Alexandre Ghiulamila 1989

Cité des Artistes

UP8, the Ciriani school of modernism, is strong in Paris. Kagan was a student of Ciriani, and Ciriani was a student in the generation of '68, still the core of the Parisian architectural establishment, some of whom worked in Le Corbusier's atelier, most of whom follow his tenets ... and so the family tree of influence unfolds. This school has bred a neo-Corbusian trend epitomised by certain clichés: monochrome white, the obsessive horizontal, curve-with-ramp, feature cuts, generous glass space, all with a hint of art deco liner – a French version of national rather than international modernism. But while this 'white look' once had an overtly socialist purpose, it has now been acquired as an image, a pastiche cubism consumed by commercial developers like a proliferating white Lego.

Cité des Artistes is genuine in its address to the character of each face of an elbow site. On rue Leblanc the white stucco runs defensively flush with the street, in stand-off with the rough stone wall of the embankment opposite and the unrelenting *hôtel industriel* by Chemetov and Huidobro beyond. The rue St-Charles façade selects an appropriate scale of openings, testing its own blend of modernism against the neighbouring residences and framing up a layered slip-route into the public Jardin Noir. The hypotenuse opens out views employing a maximum of fenestration with balcony access. Apartments overlook the Parc André-Citroën (see page 196), the glittering Cacoub carbuncle, towards the Seine and the Paris skyline.

Housing 38 north-lit studios for artists in three interlaced blocks – square, circle and triangle – the ground level is freed in parts by *piloti*. These enable a weaving of circulation: pathways and passages, earthbound and aerial, between captured courtyards. If academic, this building nevertheless has some impressive moments, for instance the gangways on the north-east side of the long bar, which Kagan calls his 'cathedral'. The

15ème arrondissement

Michel Kagan 1992

Michel Kagan 1992

plans of the studios and apartments are all different, and appear to match well the requirements of the artists.

If one accepts the Corb-collage genre, this building is good, if overworked. There are too many kinds of windows, too many slots, too many undulating screens and too many punctures in these screens, and bridges, and balconies … To be appreciated, Cité des Artistes should be understood as French high modernism (like high gothic). It is probably the best product of the Ciriani school.

ADDRESS 69 rue Leblanc, 230 rue St-Charles, 15e
CLIENT Ville de Paris
MANDATAIRE RIVP
AMENAGEUR SEMEA XV
BET structure, Batiserf
CONTRACTOR Dumez
CONTRACT VALUE FF42.8
million (1992)
SIZE 8285 square metres
net; 1300 square metres
parking
METRO Balard
ACCESS none

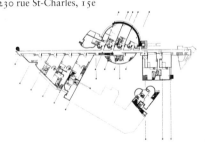

15ème arrondissement

Michel Kagan 1992

Michel Kagan 1992

Parc André-Citroën

196

The site, formerly occupied by the Citroën automobile factory, has been turned into a park of monumental scale. Its central axis invites comparison to the Jardin des Plantes, Les Invalides or the Champs de Mars, all of which are pointed towards the Seine without actually bordering it. However, the axial relationships in Parc André-Citroën fail to culminate satisfactorily at any point – the Seine is as hidden as a haha.

In this park ZAC the various adept contributors are confined within orthogonal territories. The gardens Blanc and Noir combine evergreens, granite and pleasantness with funereal care. The Jardin Sériel dabbles with alchemical themes of change and colour symbolism, but the magic and mystery are neutralised by allotment neatness. However, there is a tract of wilderness where wildflowers and weeds flourish among the leaf litter. Most popular, and impressively architectural, is the peristyle of fountains that perform in catch-you-out sequences between the two large greenhouses.

ADDRESS quai André-Citroën, rue Balard, 15e
LANDSCAPE ARCHITECTS Jardin Noir and Jardin Blanc, Alain Provost; Jardin Sériel, Gilles Clément
ZAC Citroën-Cévennes
CLIENT Ville de Paris/Direction des Parcs, Jardins et Espaces Verts
AMENAGEUR SEMEA XV
ETUDE URBAINE APUR
BET general, SGTE; greenhouses, RFR
CONTRACT VALUE FF388 million
SIZE 14 hectares
METRO Balard/RER Boulevard Victor
ACCESS open

15ème arrondissement

Jean-Paul Viguier, Jean-François Jodry, Patrick Berger 1992

15ème arrondissement

Jean-Paul Viguier, Jean-François Jodry, Patrick Berger 1992

Canal+ offices

Meier's obsession with white comes undiluted from the modernist language of the 1930s. Originally it symbolised openness, democracy even, operating to unify elements and release a flow of space. Marketed evangelically, its bloodless puritanical superiority has dominated architecture since its invention.

Meier gives all the elements in his buildings a cover-all application of whiteness. The reflectivity of white, a non-colour, means it works with light to erase material differences and so dissolve spatial boundaries. The rigidity of the forms, amplified by this whiteness, echoes the meringue shirts and wide white smiles of the American curtain-wall contractors who make buildings such as these.

Meier manipulates the modernist architectural language using a palette of developer materials and methods: panels and prefabrication. While his artful manipulations bring a certain nobility to the cheap, common materials he uses, he is nevertheless a commercial architect. He mass produces an 'intellectual' aesthetic, profiting from the projection of a distinctive image in the same way as one might brand a product. This style appeals to institutions such as Canal+, the first privately owned alternative television channel in France, which screens 80 per cent of new films less than six months after their release.

Like the American Center (see page 154), Canal+ faces both street and park, and is about the same distance from the river. The building responds to the scale of the *arrondissement* that spills from Parc André-Citroën towards the périphérique on one side and presents a height and density of façade to ward off the concrete tower-fest that disfigures the Front de Seine on the other. Its role as a city-structuring mass is similar to, if less bombastic than, that of the finance ministry (see page 146).

Seine side, employees see the river through ribbons of square train-

Richard Meier and Partners 1992

Richard Meier and Partners 1992

carriage windows. At the back, the regulatory set-back demands break down the bulk to a more penetrable volume, using the same language articulated at a domestic scale. Here the building surrounds a little local park, home to a coterie of cats.

The studios and production workshops are in the bar of building that runs along rue des Cévennes. Above and behind, conference rooms and the staff restaurant lie under the aeroplane-wing roof, overlooking the park at the back. The administration division occupies the seven-storey offices overlooking the Seine. These are built against a slicing 'wall' which frames up the Meier 'window on the world'. This rectangular void overlooks Paris, with a (probably stunning) view available only to satellite-dish cleaners. For most, it performs as a cut-out sky-stencil. The entrance, at the junction of the two buildings, leads into a large atrium. Dangerous detailing (falling panels) has resulted in an expanse of white netting being draped, like the bridal cobwebs of Miss Havisham, over the façades.

This building is a variation on a theme, an expedience to be expected of commercial architecture. Higher Meier (or Meier+) is better expressed in his museums in Atlanta and Frankfurt.

Don't miss the calligraphic balconies of Bassompierre, de Rutte and Sirvin (1936) nearby at 7 rond-point du Pont Mirabeau.

ADDRESS quai André-Citroën and 2 rue des Cévennes, 15e
CLIENT Canal+
ARCHITECT CORRESPONDANT Jean Mas
CLIENT DELEGUE Cogédim Aménagement
SIZE 45,000 square metres
METRO Javel/Balard
ACCESS none

Richard Meier and Partners 1992

Richard Meier and Partners 1992

Pont de Bir-Hakeim

By day the city structure of Paris is unreadable. Monuments merge into the mass of the city fabric, paths and landmarks are camouflaged by the wealth of visual information.

By night, however, the structure of the city can be read through its lighting. An aerial view of Paris clearly reveals the hierarchy of systems: the compact mass of buildings tied into a rough circle by the pinky-orange lights of the périphérique, the key structuring lines of most intense light defining the avenues and boulevards which lead to *places* and monuments bathed in light (switched off at 1.00). Most distinctive are the absences of light, the voids that denote parks and cemeteries. Other elements, such as bridges, have an ambiguous character. Should they light their surroundings or should they be lit?

These questions confronted Fortier, Rota and Bonnet in their re-evaluation, through lighting, of the Pont de Bir-Hakeim. Formerly called the Viaduc de Passy (1903–06) and designed by engineer Louis Biette, architect J-C Formigé and sculptor Gustave Michel, this is a double bridge, the upper part being used by the métro. It spans between the 15e and 16e *arrondissements*, pausing to touch the tip of the linear island, allée des Cygnes.

Analysis of the importance of this bridge as a landmark on the Seine and as a work of art indivisible from its context determined the decision to light the entire structure as a monument in a manner similar to the Eiffel Tower. This has been achieved by breaking down the whole into a series of parts which require subtle and differentiated treatments within the overall scheme. Families of elements have been identified – stone plinth and copings, metal structure and decorations, architecture and topography of the banks, the métro. Each part has been evaluated for its role with respect to lighting within the total composition.

15ème arrondissement

Bruno Fortier and Italo Rota with Frédéric Bonnet 1995–

Bruno Fortier and Italo Rota with Frédéric Bonnet 1995–

The road level of the bridge was originally lit by pendant lanterns hung from the métro viaduct; these are to be reinstated, giving an intermittent intensity of light on the middle level. The masonry foundations and ornamental motifs will be washed with light, creating a halo effect at the springing point of the arches supporting the roadway. The bridge will be moored between the banks by discrete lighting of the towers that bracket the passage of the métro. Above and independent from this glowing organisation is a contrasting aleatory dynamic: the métro will be placed in the cross-fire of projectors. This lighting will remain imperceptible until the train, zipping over, slips between the beams.

Beware the *bateaux mouches* – floating stadia equipped with floodlights which vacuum up the shadows of the river façades.

15ème arrondisement

ADDRESS between rue de
l'Alboni and boulevard
de Grenelle, 15e
CLIENT Direction de
l'Aménagement Urbain/
Direction de la Voirie/RATP
METRO Bir-Hakeim/Passy
ACCESS open

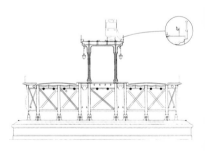

Bruno Fortier and Italo Rota with Frédéric Bonnet 1995–

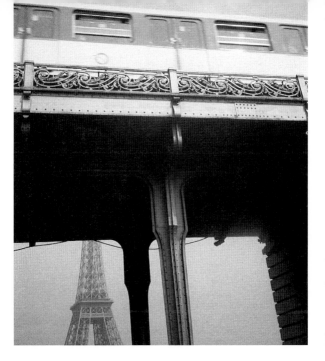

Bruno Fortier and Italo Rota with Frédéric Bonnet 1995–

16ème–18ème arrondissements

Funicular

For the price of a métro ticket, the funicular at Montmartre delivers the joyrider on to the lap of the saccharine Sacré Coeur, offering an ascending view over Paris on the way.

The funicular is placed lightly and unobtrusively to the west side of the Montmartre hill. Meticulous refinement of the components has resulted in a taut membrane of glass held at its extremities by a double bracket set at the tips of the structural arms. The steel and glass interlock mechanically, using a principle similar to bone and flesh which is both flexible and resistant: this maintains a system of strain and balance. There is no intermediary linking structure between the arms and the membrane. Note the dextrous centimetres of woven-steel drainpipe that circumvent a tricky junction.

The glass stations hover minimally, top and bottom. Steel is detailed to extinction, leaving the glass canopy wings to hang pterodactyl-like over the track – a modern reinterpretation of Guimard's art nouveau glass-and-iron canopy for nearby métro Abbesses. The sleek cabins sport the dynamic lines and muted lustre of seductive industrial-design gadgetry. You just have to ride one.

ADDRESS place Suzanne-Valadon and
rue du Cardinal-Dubois, 18e
CLIENT RATP
CABIN DESIGN Roger Tallon
BET Marc Malinowsky
CONTRACT VALUE FF15 million
SIZE each glass canopy 200 square metres
METRO Abbesses/Anvers
ACCESS public transport

16ème–18ème arrondissements

François Deslaugier 1990

François Deslaugier 1990

Secteur Goutte d'Or

Men from every nation were there, Ligurians, Lusitanians, Balearics, Negroes and fugitives from Rome. You could hear besides the heavy Doric dialect the Celtic syllables ringing out like battle chariots, and Ionic endings clashed with desert consonants, harsh as jackal-cries. Greeks could be recognised by their slender figures, Egyptians by their hunched shoulders, Cantabrians by their sturdy calves. Cairns proudly tossed their helmet plumes, Cappadocians had painted great flowers on their bodies with herbal juices, and some Lydians in woman's dress wore slippers and earrings as they dined. Others who had daubed themselves ceremoniously with vermilion looked like coral statues.
Gustave Flaubert, *Salammbô* (1862), translated by A J Krailsheimer

This was Flaubert's Goutte d'Or, a popular *faubourg* of Paris which throughout its history has been an area of dense immigration. For several years it has been the subject of a contentious renovation. Certain buildings deemed unstable or insalubrious have been demolished, others have been repaired and made habitable. A scattering of new projects has been inserted in the toothless gaps in the building fabric. Some are sensitive to the culture and delicate scale of the *quartier*, with its faultline passageways, stairs and lightwells, while others gatecrash, big, brash and brand new.

A group of local inhabitants has campaigned to have this upgrading operation monitored, so as to protect the distinctive physical and social characteristics of the area. Fortunately this seems to have warded off some of the more zealous purging. Regardless, the district is delineated forever in the literary memory of Parisians as the home of the wretched slum dwellers of Zola's novel *L'Assommoir* of 1872, which follows the tragic life of Gervaise through drunkenness, promiscuity, filth and starvation.

16ème–18ème arrondissements

Various architects 1984–

Various architects 1984–

The Goutte d'Or is an area to walk around, savouring the unique character and variety of merchandise bequeathed by the rich ethnic mix of its inhabitants. The choice between preservation, conservation, demolition and substitution is an issue faced by many European cities. What is progress and at what price?

ADDRESS area bounded by boulevard de la Chapelle, boulevard Barbes, rue Polonceau and rue de Jessaint, 18e
CLIENT OPAC/Ville de Paris
SIZE 7-hectare *quartier*: rehabilitation of 600 ancient dwellings, construction of 800 new dwellings
ACCESS views from street only

Various architects 1984–

Various architects 1984–

19ème arrondissement

Apartments for post-office employees

The street frontage is unexpectedly set back and unzipped. The act goes against the Parisian convention of the continuous, planar street façade, and the provocative gap suggests the presence of the usually hidden court-yard behind. The paired box-like buildings scissor with the tense intimacy of a tango.

Right angles, orthogonal cross-passes and juxtapositions construct a balanced spatial equation. Horizontal metal shutters move against the vertical wooden ladder panels; the open stair pushes backwards and forwards, launching diving-board balconies, returns and returns again to face the street – an interrelationship of static parts that produces a result as fluid as any baroque building.

19ème arrondissement

ADDRESS 46 rue de l'Ourcq, 19e
CLIENT SA HLM Toit et Joie
SIZE 1672 square metres
BUREAU D'ETUDES BET C Ferm
METRO Crimée
ACCESS none

Philippe Gazeau 1994

Philippe Gazeau 1994

Quai de la Loire apartments

19ème arrondissement

This vast and magnificent tenement, among the finest contemporary housing in Paris, takes up a whole city block by the side of the bassin de la Villette. Girard, who studied and taught at UP8, won the RIVP competition in 1982. Her project displays an ingenuity that is political as much as spatial, practical, tactical and imaginative.

It was the matrix of constraints governing the project that supplied the raw material. The Paris building regulations controlled the heights and massing – a seven-storey height restriction coded the canal frontage, while a six-storey limit was imposed on the other three sides. Then there was the precise orientation of the site – north-west–south-east – which determined the distribution of sunlight, prevailing wind and views. Add to this the location of this near-rectangular block: bounded by two slim streets at the sides, fronting the open tow path and canal and backing on to a sports ground-cum-park in a neighbourhood whose living patterns involve work and leisure, shops, transport, squares and favourite routes. Then throw into the equation a meagre budget.

Girard's considerate response to these constraints, balancing physical, legal and social requirements with some witty morsels for the academics, has created a project that reaches beyond the intellectual accolades of other architects (of which there have been many) to the people who live within its walls.

The building is divided into two Ls, each of which takes up two sides of the site, cupping a courtyard between them. This runs from canal corner to street corner, from an opening that frames a view of Ledoux's rotunda at the end of the basin to another opposite Gaudin's excellent extension to the school building, Collège Tandou. These entry/exit points, between the Ls, provide full-height slits which allow sunlight to penetrate the inner garden from east and west. The undulating glass wall of the

Edith Girard 1985

19ème arrondissement

Edith Girard 1985

conciergerie by the entry point on the west side provides a marvellous introduction to the elevations of the courtyard. This space is modelled in such a way as to avoid excessive overlooking and to encourage the reception of sunlight on all façades, internal and external. The apartments open out on to sun-seeking balconies.

The façades of the L to south-west and south-east are thoughtfully scaled, divided into base, middle and top sections, each assertively articulated and finely detailed. The tallest part of the building presents an elevation of some presence to the canal, while the east side has windows that side-step out along the angled street so that these apartments too have a view of the water.

Careful use is made of different rendering techniques – stucco, grey paint and pebbles – contrasting horizontal and vertical emphases and differentiating between constituent parts of the façade. The grey concrete of the five-storey-plus base is teased from above by the expressive phrasing of the penthouses, scantily clad in red, blue and green tiles.

19ème arrondissement

ADDRESS 64 quai de la Loire, 19e
CLIENT RIVP
SIZE 111 apartments
METRO Laumière
ACCESS none

Edith Girard 1985

Edith Girard 1985

City Cleaning Depot

A depot for storing and repairing the city's street-cleaning equipment that might have been relegated, along with the refuse, to an out-of-the-way shed has been transformed by Piano into a delicately worked industrial shop window. Smooth and refined, the façade seems to contradict the supposedly ignoble pursuits that go on behind it. But to remind us what the building is for, all the metallic components – supporting structures, staircases and guard rails – are in galvanised steel, the material used for the large dustbins dragged out by *concierges* from the buildings of Paris each morning, until it was replaced by wheelie-bin plastic.

The building offers plenty of ideas for those interested in clever detailing. The horizontal sheets of glass are clipped to a supporting structure of rectangular-section steel tubes, internal sills to pots of geraniums. The language of planar surfaces is set off by the fine metal verticals and horizontals. At the scale of building composition, the depot is a wonderfully three-dimensional object. The sheer wall is relieved by attachments: metal staircases, lift mechanism, entrance canopy and railings that guard the drop into the dry fronting moat. North light and views penetrate the double-volume workshops below. The extraordinary lighting mast in front is an industrial sculpture – allowed a few curves – housing the motor to pull open one of the gates.

The south-facing yard façade uses quite another vocabulary. Set back from the street, it is made up of bright red enamelled-metal panels, colouring in the exposed grid of a precast-concrete skeleton. The system creates courtyards which allow light into the deepest recesses of the building.

On either side of Piano's building are two *hôtels industriels* (see page 168). To the right, Jodry and Viguier's Metropole 19 (1988) is sleek and futuristic, carefully detailed with a passionate austerity reminiscent of

19ème arrondissement

Renzo Piano Building Workshop 1989

Eero Saarinen's General Motors Technical Center of 1956. To the left, the vertical light-catching slot of Gazeau's Cuisine Centrale Curial (1989) plays shiny handrail diagonals against horizontal corrugations, with a *soupçon* of the cooks stirring inside. When the three buildings are considered together, one realises that, very unusually, an entire contemporary industrial street has been inserted into the city.

19ème arrondissement

ADDRESS 17 rue Raymond Radiguet, 19e
CLIENT Ville de Paris/RIVP
BET GEC
CONTRACTOR Dumez
METRO Crimée
ACCESS none

Renzo Piano Building Workshop 1989

Renzo Piano Building Workshop 1989

Cité des Sciences et de l'Industrie

After a certain size, bigness or XL can be understood only as a comparison, a building up of scales with which we are familiar. This old abattoir is approximately equal to four Centres Pompidou, the Centre Pompidou is equal to five Arcs de Triomphe, and so on.

The basic frame was the world's largest white elephant, the bare and uncompleted hulk of what was to have been the most up-to-date metropolitan abattoir in the history of abattoirs – before it was realised that the advent of the refrigerated lorry made it unnecessary to bring live cattle into the city for slaughter. Work stopped.

The vast mid-nineteenth-century building, a more-or-less isolated, freestanding object on the site of the Parc de la Villette (see page 234), had all the problems of a non-purpose-designed exhibition hall. The installation designers carried the Herculean responsibility of creating a cohesive image for the museum as a whole: a rapport between displays and container. Their work was invariably dwarfed, so, daunted, they retreated to conventional display techniques which lack the pioneering zeal necessary to engage the discrepancies of scale.

The abattoir skeleton consists of four rows of twinned seven-storey-high columns carrying monstrous trusses that clear span over spaces each only slightly smaller than the plan of the Centre Pompidou. The megalith is further fortified by a moat. Fainsilber's *parti* is conventional relative to what a Gehry or a Rogers might have done: there are no unexpected jim-crack diagonals breaking through the exterior or disembowelled guts (services and circulation) displayed on the outside. Instead Fainsilber's intervention is entirely internal, symmetrical and orthogonal – the museum is a vast top-lit stairwell.

Stairs are what one might expect to find as the central feature of any major capital-city museum, even if traditional staircases have been

Adrien Fainsilber 1987

Adrien Fainsilber 1987

replaced by escalators. Here, however, the ascent lacks the magical view of Beaubourg or the surprise emergence on to the street from the métro underworld. This ride is more in department-store mode: merely functional, though very shiny.

The huge glazed bays of the Grandes Serres designed by Peter Rice (see page 230) are to be found on the south side at the back. As with all brilliant innovations, it is hard to recognise what the innovation actually is and realise its importance, not least because it has been much copied. These vessels, large and beautiful, seem functionless – only one of the great green glasshouses holds plants.

Fainsilber had originally prepared a Beaux-Arts plan for the park, with a central axis that now runs only as far as the Géode (his plans were superseded by the Tschumi park, see page 234). The Géode, a hemispherical-screen cinema, is clad in triangular steel mirror plates which produce suitably weird reflections of the surroundings, accompanied by the gurgle of sci-fi water music which issues forth from the often-empty pool on which the metallic ball rests.

ADDRESS 30 avenue Corentin Cariou, 19e
CLIENT Etablissement Public du Parc de la Villette
ENGINEER RFR
CONTRACTOR GTM
SIZE 30,000 square metres of exhibition space
METRO Porte de la Villette
ACCESS open every day except Monday, 10.00–18.00

Adrien Fainsilber 1987

19ème arrondissement

Adrien Fainsilber 1987

Grandes Serres

> It is a study of the nature of the structure, rather than the nature of the image, which yields the greatest puzzle and the greatest satisfaction when it is understood.
> Peter Rice, *An Engineer Imagines*, 1994

In September 1980 Fainsilber, who had just won the competition for the Cité des Sciences et de l'Industrie (see page 226), invited engineer Peter Rice to design the Grandes Serres or giant greenhouses at the back of the museum overlooking the Parc de la Villette. With Martin Francis and Ian Ritchie, Rice formed RFR, a small group of architects and engineers that was to become his private research office in Paris.

The museum was intended to be an example of French industry at its best. Fainsilber had been inspired by Norman Foster's Willis Faber Dumas building in Ipswich, its suspended glass-wall system designed by Martin Francis with supplier Pilkington Glass. His brief for RFR was to make the greenhouses as transparent as possible, with minimum obstruction of the view of the park. The Willis Faber Dumas precedent used an all-glass façade with glass fins as mullions. But at La Villette, it was decided that the views would be obscured by fins and RFR looked instead for a solution using transoms, with a minimal visual presence. Cable trusses were adopted as the most suitable structural concept.

The use of cable trusses implied particular detailing for the glass connections. Experience at Willis Faber Dumas gave the designers confidence in the capacity of the glass to adapt to a bracing structure with significant deformation. The glass is suspended as a curtain, each pane being hung from the one above, using small vertical connections fixed to bolts in the corners of each pane. The bolts are countersunk with the heads flush with the outer plane. These bolts employ spherical bearings

Adrien Fainsilber, RFR 1987

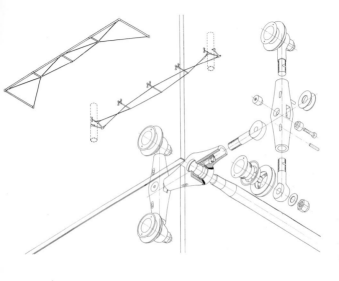

19ème arrondissement

Adrien Fainsilber, RFR 1987

– *rotules* – in their heads to ensure that any deflections of the glass or cable-truss system do not create local bending effects in the glass.

The bearings guaranteed that the glass was always loaded predictably and that it was possible to calculate accurately the maximum load that might need to be transferred. The small surface contact between the bearings and the glass exploits the glass's high local strength. Even though the diameter of each bearing is only 32 millimetres and the glass is only 12 millimetres thick, the capacity of this bearing is approximately 4 tonnes, many times the maximum load it would be expected to carry in use. The detailing was shaped by an understanding of the properties of the glass; in this respect the Grandes Serres was considered by Rice to be the project which helped him to develop an approach towards the use of materials in many schemes that followed – the Lloyd's Building, the Menil Museum, the Pyramide Inversée (page 24), Japan Bridge (page 292), the station interconnection at Roissy airport, and Kansai airport.

The Rice roof at Roissy, well worth visiting, is a 'transposition of the image of levitation'. Each structural system is expressed as an independent layer and is completely detached from the façades. Fritted-glass panels appear to float on articulated struts which are supported on croissant beams – a strong, curved bottom boom and a thin tensile top chord. These in turn are supported on fan-shaped pylons.

ADDRESS Cité des Sciences et de l'Industrie, 30 avenue Corentin Cariou, 19e
CLIENT Etablissement Public du Parc de la Villette
CONTRACTOR Eiffel
METRO Porte de la Villette
ACCESS open

Adrien Fainsilber, RFR 1987

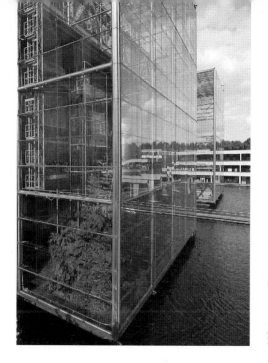

19ème arrondissement

Adrien Fainsilber, RFR 1987

Parc de la Villette

Gathered around the edges of the périphérique is an unkempt fringe of parks, cemeteries, stadia, emporia, railway land, markets, lycées and the Cité Universitaire. The site for the Parc de la Villette is on this urban/suburban circuit. An articulate competition brief put forward the idea of a park for the twenty-first century, posing the question of the nature of an urban park and its role in the city. In May 1982 Mitterrand announced Swiss architect Bernard Tschumi as winner from the 472 entries. Runner up: the OMA team headed by Rem Koolhaas.

Tschumi eschewed any suggestion of creating a pastiche rural setting that would shut out the city and the périphérique. Instead, his interests lie in the power of urban reality, in the order behind the apparent chaos and discontinuity of modern life. The Parc de la Villette deals directly with contemporary cityness, avoiding a sentimental imitation of the narrow streets and neighbourhood squares of the pre-industrial era, or the green cosmetic solutions applied to the leftover spaces around arbitrarily placed towers and slabs. It is an index to the ring of 'culture' developing in the unloved peripheral zone.

No matter how intelligent the layout of any building (and Tschumi refers to his park as a huge discontinuous building), its success depends on how it is used. The open-air 'cultural spaces' of Parc de la Villette are supposed to model city life in a state of constant transformation: 'their architecture and organisation desire not to conform or shape ideas, but reinforce, activate and intensify them, producing unimagined events'. Prosaic observation reveals the park to be a pleasant place to kick a ball or eat sandwiches at lunchtime: it is in fact one of the few parks in Paris where you are allowed to sit and walk on the grass.

The architectural strategy of the park is formed by the encounter of three autonomous systems, each with its own logic, peculiarities and

Bernard Tschumi 1993

Bernard Tschumi 1993

limits: the system of objects; the system of movements; the system of spaces. The superimposition or 'transprogramming' of these systems results in spaces and events of variable size and character producing a carefully staged series of tensions that enhances the dynamism of the park. These systems correspond to the following elements:

Surfaces These serve activities needing large horizontal spaces. Each surface is programmatically determined: grass surfaces are play-prairies in the Circle, Triangle, South Free Curve and West Square, with stabilised surfaces for light athletics in the East Square. 'Left over' surfaces, composed of compacted earth and gravel, allow 'programmatic freedom'.

Lines Two routes, perpendicular to one another, suggest the x and y axes of a graph against which the rest of the park is organised. North–south links the two Paris gates and subway stations; east–west the long ramp-bridge joins Paris to its suburbs above the Canal d'Ourcq, from which the crowd ogles the crowd. A curvilinear wiggling path forms a promenade of Thematic Gardens linking all the areas of the park; alleys of trees demarcate the main spaces and delineate the geometric forms: square, circle and triangle.

Points A grid of folly structures contains and locates the programmatic requirements. The generic 10-metre-square red, three-storey cubes from which the individualised follies mutate are placed at 120-metre intervals signalling point-type activities such as exhibitions, cafés, concerts and computing. The strict repetition of the basic folly becomes a symbol for the park; the grid of the follies corresponds to the columnar grid of a modern building, but unlike columns, the follies possess the status of objects activating space. That the follies are incorporated into two of the Grands Serres (see page 230) of the Cité des Sciences et de l'Industrie and provide two supports for the massive gestural girder of Portzamparc's

Bernard Tschumi 1993

19ème arrondissement

Bernard Tschumi 1993

Cité de la Musique (see page 244) is, like some of the other formal ideas, difficult to perceive unless one is armed with an axonometric diagram. It has no doubt particularly pleased Tschumi, whose follies are supposed to be empty of meaning, that the folly destined to be a kindergarten has become a TV studio, a folly garden centre was reconceived as a restaurant and is finally a painting studio, while another remains functionless.

If there is a deconstructivist architecture it is surely this – not only does Tschumi make the claim, but he is backed up by a long theoretical essay by Jacques Derrida, founder of deconstruction. Yet it is hard to credit the follies as anything more than a clever rip-off of the graphics of constructivism, with little or no original plastic value in themselves. If this is so, Tschumi's main contribution is the invisible bit. It would seem timely to ask a naïve question: is this Emperor of Deconstruction wearing any clothes?

FOLLY a building in the form of a castle, temple, etc., built to satisfy a fancy or conceit, often of an eccentric kind.
Dictionary definition

ADDRESS Porte de la Villette, avenue Jean-Jaurès, 19e
CLIENT Etablissement Public du Parc de la Villette
SIZE 55 hectares
METRO Porte de Pantin/Porte de la Villette
ACCESS open

19ème arrondissement

Bernard Tschumi 1993

19ème arrondissement

Bernard Tschumi 1993

Jardin des Bambous

Article L 110 of the French Town Planning Code states the obvious: The French territory is the common heritage of the nation … The question 'how do we train for town planning?' has always intrigued me. Mightn't gardens be the best place to learn about mastering the forms of a city? Like the city, gardens always escape from form. Like the city, gardens are occupied, they are places where use comes into being, where things change in the course of the seasons and in time. There is always some part of a project that escapes from its instigator; the idea of the project itself becomes relative.

Alexandre Chemetoff, translated by Armelle Lavalou, *L'Architecture d'Aujourd'hui*, no. 303, February 1996

Footbridges above this excavated garden map the sewage pipes of the city network and continue the folly-gridded gameboard of Parc de la Villette (see page 234). A green anti-clockwise descent mirrors the red clockwise ascent of the adjacent folly. Originally titled 'Garden of Energy', its sheltered, sun-warmed 120-metre concrete wall releases heat at night to encourage 40 species of bamboo to grow. There is an eerie scalelessness to this mad weed – grass or tree?

19ème arrondissement

ADDRESS Parc de la Villette, 19e
CLIENT Etablissement Public du Parc de la Villette
SIZE 3000 square metres
COST FF2700 per square metre (1987)
METRO Porte de Pantin/Port de la Villette
ACCESS open

Alexandre Chemetoff 1987

Alexandre Chemetoff 1987

Chairs (Parc de la Villette)

If somebody wanted an ordinary chair he or she had to go to the flea market to find one. I certainly don't want to encourage this trend, so I started wondering what a chair is like ... So I produce something in which everybody has a memory, as if I already had the mould into which the plastic is to be poured ... When you unveil it, some people recognise it, though it didn't exist before. But at the same time it was always there.

Philippe Starck interviewed by Federica Zanco, *Domus* 1991

Lightly touching the earth on a point pivot, stiffened by a single spinal fin, the folds and curves of Starck's chairs at La Villette combine to soften the steely planes. Placed seemingly accidentally yet as precisely as the *Blade Runner* origami figures, the members of the windswept group turn to address each other.

Neither architect nor industrial designer, Starck prefers to call himself 'a producer of fertile surprises'. His focus is on function, but from a different viewpoint. He takes quality of technique and technology as a given and uses as his point of departure the emotional meaning the objects communicate, their hidden purpose. He suggests that the main, perhaps the only, direction for designers to work in is to attempt to answer Lamartine's question: 'Do inanimate objects have a soul?'

ADDRESS Porte de la Villette, avenue Jean-Jaurès, 19e
CLIENT Etablissement Public du Parc de la Villette
METRO Porte de Pantin/Porte de la Villette
ACCESS open

19ème arrondissement

Philippe Starck 1993

19ème arrondissement

Philippe Starck 1993

Cité de la Musique

> A city is a vast colloquium of ever more diverse epochs, strata and objects that stack up and integrate with a blend of freedom and a set of rules rather than according to some idea of homogeneity.
> Christian de Portzamparc, from the introduction to *Guide to Modern Architecture in Paris* by Hervé Martin, 1991

This périphérique-scale project dominates the eastern stretch of avenue Jean-Jaurès. In the manner of all large institutions, it is a city in itself, with boroughs, neighbourhoods and departments determined by the political architecture of academic territories and alliances.

The project is organised in two asymmetrical parts which integrate with the existing buildings, *places* and objects – including the Parc de la Villette (see page 234), the renovated Grande Halle, the Lion fountain and the surrounding city – in a sophisticated composition. Portzamparc started by restructuring the spatial relationships between these pieces by creating a great external vestibule which also acts as a gate or window within the wall of buildings fronting the park. Here the first Tschumi folly is used as an antechamber between the city and the park.

Portzamparc's approach to architecture draws on the idea that a building is a fragment of city, embodying the characteristic scales and densities of urban living. His perspective on the city acknowledges all its states of being and epochs in the knowledge that just as it will never all be torn down, neither will it ever all be modern. The commission for the Cité de la Musique was a large enough project for him to test out his vocabulary of city-type spaces, and though his representation of the city within this complex rejects archetypal urban forms such as literal streets and squares, spaces that perform comparable social functions are none-theless present.

Christian de Portzamparc, first phase 1990, second phase 1994

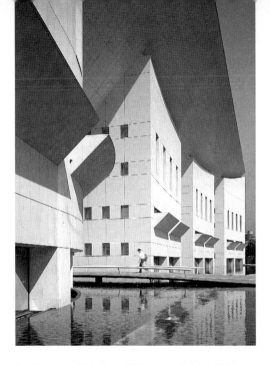

Christian de Portzamparc, first phase 1990, second phase 1994

Portzamparc uses a hybrid of modern styles made up of tensions, dialogues and dynamics plagiarised from the surrounding urban disorder grafted on to plum gestures from Le Corbusier's *Œuvre Complète* – spot the chimney from Firminy and bits of La Tourette. A sniff of 1930s curvilinear ocean liner is performed upon by a random geometry to achieve articulated fragments. The result presumes to conjure up the crevices and corners, alleys and overhangs of formal city planning corrupted by dwellers over centuries – to arrive at a familiar idiosyncratic complexity in four years instead of 400. The huge, very white marzipan shapes squiggle together in a disturbing marriage of styles, processed into an unmistakable family of elements. Tschumi's wavy *galerie* wiggles by, up to the same tricks but in metal not masonry.

The two contrasting but complementary complexes were determined through a brief devised in discussion with composer-director Pierre Boulez. The western wing, approximately rectilinear in plan, consists of a reasonably dense group of buildings containing rehearsal rooms for students, teaching and performance, with residential accommodation for the National Music Conservatoire. The shallow curving entrance bridge leads into a multiple-volume space: lounge below, balcony above, with views through and out. Openings frame Tschumi's red follies and the prim elevations of Rossi's housing next door (see page 250).

The courtyard enclosure is bizarrely space-age, with strange projectiles framing a multi-dimensional intersection of outdoor levels, stages, arenas and platforms in which disembodied toots engage with half-heard conversations and traffic rumbles. The large conical recital room, beneath what looks like a streamlined ship's funnel, has ceilings that soar upwards into the cone-shaped roof, panelled with timber in a pattern that resembles the roof of the Pantheon. It is an almost ritualistic space

Christian de Portzamparc, first phase 1990, second phase 1994

Christian de Portzamparc, first phase 1990, second phase 1994

– the concert platform like the altar and the audience a congregation.

The eastern wing is wedge shaped in plan and addresses the space around the Lion fountain with a triangular addition that defines a new diagonal axis into the park. It contains major public facilities: a large elliptical concert hall around which spirals an ammonoid lobby; the national museum of musical instruments; a music teaching centre; and a centre of experimental music. In this wing Portzamparc has chosen to integrate a folly of his own design.

The jury is still out on Pritzker-prized Portzamparc: is he simply a stylist or is his architecture of such significance it will change people's lives? He is also responsible for the Holiday Inn across the road …

ADDRESS 21 avenue Jean-Jaurès, 19e
CLIENT Etablissement Public du Parc de la Villette/Ministère de la Culture et de la Communication/Direction de la Musique
SCENOGRAPHIE Dubreuil
BET acoustics, Sodeteg, Sogeleg–Commins
CONTRACTOR SGE TPI
CONTRACT VALUE FF207 million (1984)
SIZE 40,000 square metres (rentable area)
METRO Porte de Pantin
ACCESS open

Christian de Portzamparc, first phase 1990, second phase 1994

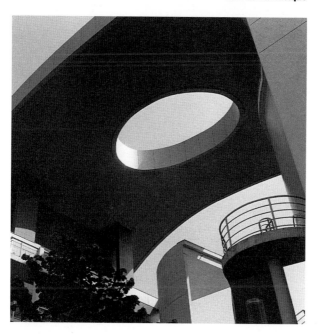

19ème arrondissement

Christian de Portzamparc, first phase 1990, second phase 1994

Avenue Jean-Jaurès housing

Admirably, this is not an object building. The architect's intention is to create a block that will blend over time into the patterns and patinas of the neighbourhood. This project parades many of Aldo Rossi's preoccupations: sensuous austerity, planar rationality and Platonic volumes. The last urban block before the Parc de la Villette and the périphérique, its relentlessly aligned façade is pierced by passageways which reach through to the closed courtyard and its interior garden. Echoing his colonnades at Modena and the arch-and-column passageways of the rue de Rivoli, a perimeter arcade draws attention to the ground floor and the importance of the street, though it still awaits occupation by colourful and lively shops.

The forms employ materials and techniques that reflect well-observed details of the locality. The main buildings are surfaced in stucco, a traditional finish to traditional prefabricated construction in concrete and masonry. The roofs are also traditional, clad in zinc and galvanised steel. The 'head' of the building is in stone, a grey or light yellow copying an eighteenth-century French palette. Innate to the Italian confidence is a sensuous enjoyment of colour – the cylindrical corner-post office is in zaffre.

Just as Rossi's floating theatre in Venice was, marvellously, like a bit of Venice floating, this housing block moors Parisian building culture, within a modern interpretation, within Paris.

ADDRESS avenue Jean-Jaurès (next to Cité de la Musique), 19e
CLIENT SAGI – SEMAVIP
SIZE 96 apartments, shops and a post office
METRO Porte de Pantin
ACCESS to public spaces only

19ème arrondissement

Aldo Rossi and Claude Zuber 1991

Aldo Rossi and Claude Zuber 1991

Rue de Rouen crèche

After some work with a coloured pencil I succeeded in making my first drawing. My Drawing Number One … I showed my masterpiece to the grown-ups, and asked them if the drawing frightened them. But they answered: 'Frighten? Why should anyone be frightened by a hat?'

My drawing was not a picture of a hat. It was a picture of a boa constrictor digesting an elephant. But since the grown-ups were not able to understand it, I made another drawing: I drew the inside of the boa constrictor, so the grown-ups could see it clearly. They always need to have things explained. My Drawing Number Two looked like this …

From Antoine de Saint-Exupéry, *The Little Prince*

The crèche building is a typical RIVP invited-competition commission for young architectural practices. Often these buildings are made-up to look as if they are for children, but it is more probable that what is created is suited to an adult's idea of what children might like rather than what children themselves enjoy.

Typically, crèche design in Paris relies on a jokey, patronising one-liner façade behind which lies the struggle for a light-penetrated section. Journal-published crèches include: 53 rue d'Hautville, 10e, by Marc Béri and Philippe Gazeau, 1988 (a brick snipped façade); 56 rue St-Maur, 11e, by Christian Hauvette, 1990 (a defensive concrete screen); and passage Chanvin, 13e, by Olivier Chaslin, 1992 (a low white horizontal building).

The site of the Granveaud and Katz crèche is tiny. The concomitant problem was the penetration and distribution of light, particularly to the inner ground-floor areas.

The solution organised the layout on a diagonal. This avoided face-to-face confrontation with the older surrounding buildings and maximised light penetration by opening up the heart of the lot with a diagonal

Pierre Granveaud, Pablo Katz 1991

19ème arrondissement

Pierre Granveaud, Pablo Katz 1991

slot. The sharply angled entrance, between the street frontage and a lower, blue-painted undercroft, gives access through a top-lit 'alley' which cuts the nursery in two and leads through and out towards the garden. This is covered by lean-to patent glazing, making up the rift between the two sides of the building. Light is caught by various means in the gap. Floors are set back and inner transparencies maximised, with openings to court-yards and walkways along the edge. The street façade has large windows laid out in the dark sandstone, cutaways opening up to the internal circulation. The tiled surface of the front of the building is organised by linear white mortar joints into a grid of squares, jauntily broken up by different sizes of openings and grilles.

The crèche appears to be popular with grown-ups and those growing up. The pointed prow of the building culminates in a shiny boiler chimney. Does it toot?

19ème arrondissement

ADDRESS 13 bis rue de Rouen, 19e
CLIENT Ville de Paris
CLIENT REPRESENTATIVE RIVP
CONTRACTOR Sicra
CONTRACT VALUE FF8 million
SIZE 1000 square metres
METRO Riquet
ACCESS none

Pierre Granveaud, Pablo Katz 1991

Pierre Granveaud, Pablo Katz 1991

Apartments, rue de Meaux

The site at rue de Meaux was originally the City Cleaning Depot. It has been relaid out by Piano as a housing scheme surrounding the square des Bouleaux, a picturesque garden designed by Desvignes et Dalnoky.

The original depot consisted of a large backland with a relatively narrow street frontage. Before site clearance could be undertaken, a new depot had to be provided (see page 222). The land was owned by the Ville de Paris, and the commission came from the RIVP. The new housing – 220 apartments and maisonettes – was sold while design was still in progress to an insurance company, on condition that the units would be let at middle-range, controlled rents.

A spinney of silver birches delicately draws attention to the slender grey GRC mullions of the façades. As a gentle light-filtering screen, the trees also provide visual and aural privacy and reduce echo. The inner recti-linear court (66 x 25 x 25 metres high) approximates a stretch of local street. The garden can be glimpsed from the street, in Mediterranean fashion, through the gate grille.

The least interrupted, planar elevations of the building fill the gap in the rue de Meaux frontage, using matching levels and palettes to unite a rationalist building of 1898 with a stucco-fronted Parisian block. The elevations that address the land-locked courtyards typical of the area are softer. Here legal restrictions concerning daylighting angles were imposed by neighbouring buildings. The planning authorities also asked that adjoining walls be built up wherever possible to preserve the urban grain. The building reaches out to touch a neighbouring building above the service road which bounds three sides, recedes in places as stepped terraces on upper floors, or is undercut to provide covered space for depot parking at ground level. The GRC framework acts as a crisply articulated support to which a range of elements is attached: fixed louvres, PVC-

Renzo Piano Building Workshop 1991

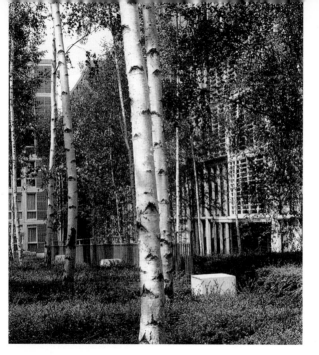

Renzo Piano Building Workshop 1991

finished window frames, tile panels, and La Poste yellow blinds. Of familiar character are the terracotta tiles cladding solid areas of the external envelope. Similar in appearance to those at IRCAM (page 72) but more crudely detailed – hung from fixings cast into the GRC panels or from battens fixed to the walls – they cost only a quarter as much.

The apartments mostly have a dual aspect, looking into the garden-park and out over the city: rue de Meaux, school playgrounds and the street-cleansing vehicle park. The maisonettes on the ground and first floors, where daylighting levels are lowest, have fully glazed façades.

This is one of the best housing schemes put up by RIVP.

ADDRESS 64, 64 bis, 64 ter rue de Meaux, 19e
CLIENT Mutuelles du Mans
ASSOCIATED ARCHITECT Bernard Plattner
LANDSCAPE ARCHITECTS Desvignes et Dalnoky
CLIENT REPRESENTATIVE RIVP
BET structure, GEC Ingénierie
CONTRACTOR Dumez
CONTRACT VALUE FF115,742,230
SIZE 20,400 square metres net; landscaping 2000 square metres
METRO Bolivar/Jaurès
ACCESS to garden only

19ème arrondissement

Renzo Piano Building Workshop 1991

Renzo Piano Building Workshop 1991

Collège Manin-Jaurès Georges Brassens

Sensibly organised, visually bizarre, this is a school. It occupies a triangular island site opening on to a playground, which in turn opens on to a square. With curves comparable to an art deco cinema, its eccentricity resides in the decoration of its walls. T-shirt-type motifs – stars, stripes, arrows, dots – are stamped out of the concrete, outwitting the material's properties as does the dextrous calligraphy of glass bends carrying neon.

Hip, dated, fun. Spot the sky-high hi-fi acroteria.

ADDRESS 51–55 rue d'Hautpoul, 19e
ZAC Manin-Jaurès
CLIENT Ville de Paris
METRO Botzaris
ACCESS none, but good view of the exterior

Manolo Nuñez-Yanowsky 1993

Manolo Nuñez-Yanowsky 1993

Allée Darius-Milhaud

Disused railway lines within Paris have provided sizeable opportunities to build – see the Opéra de la Bastille (page 128) and the Viaduc Daumesnil (page 138). Closure of the branch line to the Paris-Bestiaux goods terminus which had served the abattoirs at La Villette created a zone of redundant land ripe for redevelopment.

The chance to build a new street in the middle of a European capital city has been rare since the abandonment of the comprehensive redevelopment policies of the 1970s. Allée Darius-Milhaud, a 1-kilometre landscaped mall or walkway, links the mountainous contours of Parc des Buttes-Chaumont to the tartan plane of Parc de la Villette (see page 234). The surrounding redevelopment was intended to act as a catalyst for urban renewal between the incline of rue Manin and avenue Jean-Jaurès, creating a new neighbourhood that would interrelate both socially and formally with the existing city fabric, focused around a public space: the mall.

The Ville de Paris regeneration initiative proposed the creation of a landscaped mall, a small garden, 1000 new housing units, shops, schools, sports facilities, office accommodation, workshops and light industry. The mall and the façades overlooking it were the subject of a competition won by Sarfati, who was also commissioned to design a public nursery school bounding the mall and was appointed as co-ordinator of the 25 teams of architects who have participated in the construction of the ZAC Manin-Jaurès. These include Decq and Cornette, Bardon and Colboc (glazing curved around place Darius-Milhaud), Nuñez-Yanowsky (school with extra-terrestrial antennae, see page 260), Vasconi (housing, 44 rue d'Hautpoul), Hondelatte (school with view-impeding *brise-soleil*, 2–12 rue Goubet), and Portzamparc (commercial conglomerate Holiday Inn, avenue Jean-Jaurès).

19ème arrondissement

Alain Sarfati/AREA 1991–1994

19ème arrondissement

Alain Sarfati/AREA 1991–1994

Sarfati's mall is off beat: a slightly scruffy cross-section through a competent, if uninspiring, ZAC. Strangely theatrical gestures such as the canted stage-set wall overlooking the cemetery, the shiny metallic cuffs and headbands to the nursery school and the zodiac runes inlaid in the pavement contribute a tinsel sparkle to the predominant po-faced neo-modernism. The hit-and-miss nature of this series of urban spaces results largely from different degrees of co-operation between architects working on adjacent sites. But the park-to-park walk is well worth taking as an example of a planning process pursued with no significant change of policy since the early 1980s. It illustrates the urban objectives developed by the Ville de Paris as an alternative to the gigantism of previous modernist-inspired development which supported the demolition of entire areas, intentionally dispersing their communities, in order to rebuild from scratch at enormous social cost.

19ème arrondissement

ADDRESS boulevard Sérurier and rue Manin, 19e
CLIENT Ville de Paris/Directions de la Voirie, des Parcs, des Jardins et des Espaces Verts/SEMAVIP
ZAC Manin-Jaurès
LANDSCAPE ARCHITECT Laurence Chabrun
CONTRACTORS west section, GMT; east section Jean Lefebvre
CONTRACT VALUE FF36 million (three phases)
SIZE 18,000 square metres
METRO Ourcq/Porte de Pantin/Danube
ACCESS open

Alain Sarfati/AREA 1991–1994

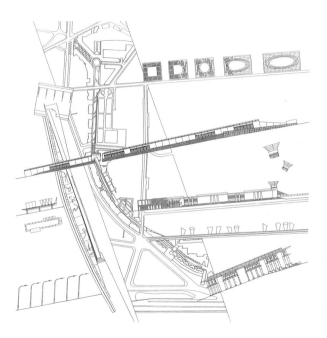

19ème arrondissement

Alain Sarfati/AREA 1991–1994

20ème arrondissement

Rue Piat apartments

Two sets of buildings, their scale echoing the pattern of the surrounding dwellings, work in a sophisticated double act to construct the park space that crowns the hill of Belleville. These buildings grow out of the steep contours, emerging as crags in a crenellated composition that creates a protective wall – a defensive retreat for the vulnerable immigrant population of this *arrondissement*.

The street façade is articulated by a complex arrangement of stairs, balcony landings and lightwells with the result that the different blocks, seen from rue Piat, look more like a group of disparate buildings than the work of a single architect. A gentle fortress.

ADDRESS 41–49 rue Piat, 20e
CLIENT RIVP
SIZE 3800 square metres
COST FF26.6 million
METRO Pyrénées
ACCESS none

Catherine Furet 1995

Catherine Furet 1995

Rue de Ménilmontant apartments

In this building Gaudin has captured the culture of the *quartier*, the informality and improvisation of the theatre of the street with its shifting wake of punters and traders, their banks of wares spilling out to blur the boundary between private and public, building and road.

The skin of the building enters into dialogue with adjacent architectural volumes and views. The façade acknowledges the existing building line and at the same time teases it. It appears to distend in rippling caresses, responding to the persuasion of occupation: the buff render wriggles and twitches to accommodate a particular glimpse or space. Elsewhere it is punctured with specific intent, bellying with promise, creviced with intrigue, responding to the unseen authority of the Parisian building codes.

That the spaces in the city – squares, streets, alleys – are as important as the buildings that frame them is acknowledged by Gaudin's courtyard, revealed through a gated opening, and the routes that filter into it. The courtyard tilts gently, with rivulet paths seeping into its corners. Half clearing, half crossroads, it echoes the matrix of alleys and passageways that characterises the area.

ADDRESS 44 rue de Ménilmontant, corner of Delaitre, 20e
CLIENT Société des Nouvelles Résidences/Ocil
SIZE 36 apartments
METRO Ménilmontant
ACCESS none

20ème arrondissement

Henri Gaudin 1987

Henri Gaudin 1987

20ème arrondissement

ZAC des Amandiers

'Le Jeu de l'Oie/Jeu de Loi, Urban Strategies for Insalubrious Islands' is a collaborative project instigated by Claire Robinson to focus attention on the plight of fragile communities threatened by large-scale commercial interests. The project's name ('The game of the goose/the game of the law') plays with the idea of a boardgame chase to defeat obstacles put up by the authorities and reach the golden goose – protection of the Amandiers.

To protect what remains of this complex urban ecology, Robinson has brought together the people of the Amandiers area and an array of volunteer architects worldwide. They have presented proposals for existing city fragments – sensitive projects of an appropriately modest nature – and described constructive ways forward for the neighbourhood.

The ZAC des Amandiers is situated in an 18-hectare zone in the northwest of the 20th *arrondissement*. Its western border is the boulevard Ménilmontant and its southern border a Haussmann avenue cut in 1870, before which the streets of the south-east sector of the zone fed into the garden outside the wall of the Père-Lachaise cemetery. The topography of the site is pronounced: a 30-metre drop from the south-east to the north-west. The popular party-wall structures negotiate the hill in steps. Formerly an important area for plaster and gypsum quarries, the ground conditions, to varying degrees stable, are qualified by numerous pockets filled with water from the now-underground River Dhuis.

These ground conditions are one of many points of contention. As the developers are not responsible for the cost of the foundation works, their records show expenses for ground-up construction only. Their monolithic developments transform the small-scale parcels of this community into large construction sites. Groups of 12 to 20 small eighteenth-century dwellings are to be replaced with a single housing block. The current plan includes restricting building heights and a vague notion of pedestrian

Claire Robinson with Archi XXe 1993–97

Claire Robinson with Archi XXe 1993–97

spaces. The gargantuan new projects erase the subtle level changes that characterise the site and tear apart the delicate urban tissue.

Over time the popular structures in masonry, wood and plaster have been taken over by the city, using a decree from the beginning of the century designed to limit 'public insalubrity'. The developer was given charge of the renewal zone with the mandate of addressing the conditions of insalubrity, but at the same time of rehabilitating certain structures chosen for their picturesque quality. Instead of studying how this could be achieved, these structures were demolished. Consequently the zone has taken on the quality of a city fragment under siege, with demolitions rampant. The buildings being systematically destroyed include 41 rue des Panoyaux, a former broom factory with a delightful central passage; 26 rue des Partants, a 'cello-maker's workshop; buildings up the hilly streets of rues Robineau, Gasnier-Guy and Mûriers; and 138 boulevard Ménilmontant, former haunt of Edith Piaf. In the ZAC des Amandiers we witness the destructive legacy of a poorly administered modern Radiant City vision. This vision – born in the post-war reconstruction era – has been transformed through bureaucracy, greed and carelessness into a movement which recreates the landscape of war from which it emerged, involving the suspension of democracy, the wholesale destruction of the urban fabric and the ravaging of communities.

ADDRESS area bounded by boulevard Ménilmontant, avenue Gambetta, rue du Sorbier, rue de Ménilmontant, 20e
CLIENT Ville de Paris
DEVELOPER AND BET SEMEA XV (appointed until 1996)
METRO Gambetta/Ménilmontant/Père-Lachaise
ACCESS open

Claire Robinson with Archi XXe 1993–97

Claire Robinson with Archi XXe 1993–97

Père-Lachaise Cemetery

This 'cemetery of the east' encompasses 47 hectares of natural hillside from which one gains views of successive cities of the living and the dead. There are tombs designed by Percier, Fontaine, Garnier, Viollet-le-Duc, Visconti, Hittorf and Davioud, and residents include the writers Proust, Balzac, Molière; composers Bizet and Chopin; artists Pissarro, Delacroix, Modigliani; and significant others Sarah Bernhardt, Oscar Wilde and Jim Morrison.

However, vandalism, graffiti and unruly tree roots have wrought considerable damage, while the proliferating garish plastic shine of the modern 'marble' tombs fails to age or blend with the soft patinated greys of its nineteenth-century bedfellows. The Ville de Paris, aware of the dangers that increasingly threaten this public retreat, has taken the first steps along the tightrope between renovation and conservation by commissioning Berger to rethink and ultimately remake the Romantic Sector, north-east of the carrefour du Grand-Rond.

A guide plan giving the positions of some of the illustrious dead is available from the keeper's lodge. If you want more ghoul, try the extraordinary architecture of the catacomb labyrinths under the street system south of the entrance at 1 place Denfert-Rochereau, 14e.

ADDRESS bounded by avenue Gambetta, rue des Rondeaux, rue de Bagnolet and boulevard Ménilmontant (main entrance), 20e
CLIENT Ville de Paris/Direction des Parcs, des Jardins et des Espaces Verts/DRAE
LANDSCAPE ARCHITECT Gilles Clément
METRO Père-Lachaise
ACCESS open 7.00–19.00

20ème arrondissement

Patrick Berger 1991–

20ème arrondissement

Patrick Berger 1991–

Apartments for post-office employees

This eye-rubbing project, in a rather staid neighbourhood, is deliciously ambiguous and irreverently lascivious.

The main idea in this building is its use of nap. Buildings, like people, are mostly seen obliquely, an attractive semi-profile glimpsed across a room among many other faces. Yet so many elevations are designed through full-flat-frontal drawings. Here an understanding of the riches of the oblique view has generated two front elevations of contrasting character – one personality encountered when walking up rue des Pyrénées, its other self when walking down.

From one direction the building presents a tall visored visage – a pair of pale curving shields with strip slots forming a shadowy ribbing: views out only. Approaching this same building from the other direction, an unexpected interior is revealed. Fleshy green tongues of building protrude from a lush orifice of crazy-paved craggy-molar balconies. This 28-metre-deep fissure provides a 4-metre gap, buffering the next-door building and allowing light to flood into the dwellings from the south. While the post office occupies the entire ground floor, its trademark *beckers jaune* is flaunted above.

ADDRESS 132 rue des Pyrénées, 20e
CLIENT Toit et Joie pour le Ministère des Postes et Télécommunications
CONTRACTOR apartments, Bouygues; post office, Nord-France
CONTRACT VALUE FF11,700 per square metre (retail)
METRO Gambetta
ACCESS post office only

Michel Bourdeau 1994

20ème arrondissement

Michel Bourdeau 1994

Beyond the périphérique

Pylons 1

Electricité de France (EDF) had the idea of running a competition to look at the aesthetics of conveying high-tension, 400,000-volt transmission lines overland on pylons. Each entry was assessed for its innovation, technical feasibility and image, including its impact on public opinion. Late-nineteenth-century engineers such as Vladimir Suchov made copious studies of the structural and formal characteristics of pylons. It seems that the schemes by joint winners Mimram and Ritchie/RFR/Gustafson (see page 284) suggest a return to modest values and formal simplicity, using forms that perhaps seem obvious, but are far from banal.

Mimram's pylons are so skinny as to be on the borderline of anorexia, drawing the eye almost uninterrupted to the horizon. Ranging from 45 to 64 metres high, they are made in three parts – body, stem and antennae – arranged as a braced pole or portico. The body is an elliptical hollow shaft of pierced cast steel, a common nineteenth-century material, that filters light as if through foliage. Mimram observed that the ideal stem would be made of glass: a simple pile of prestressed isolators on a steel body. Here, however, he proposes the stem as a steel cone made up of an assembly of cast-steel elements with an elliptical base. The antennae, made of two semi-elliptical half-shells of rolled steel and subject to the smallest structural strains, hold the earth cable.

The reed solution.

Beyond the périphérique

CLIENT Electricité de France
COST just less than three times the cost of the present cable pylons
QUANTITY 800 per year

Marc Mimram 1998

Beyond the périphérique

Marc Mimram 1998

Pylons 2

The design of the Ritchie/RFR/Gustafson pylon emerged from a inter-disciplinary perspective: the collaboration of architect, engineer and landscape architect. Given the sensitivity needed to place pylons in the landscape, the team pursued the idea of how their lines describe space rather than occupy it.

The proposal comprises a floating ribbon of six lines that reduces the silhouette of the pylon to a lowercase 'f'. This form has the capacity to divide and reconfigure in a manner similar to natural growth systems, where complex forms result from a series of repetitive units. When the conductors change direction, the two 'f's are linked to form a braced frame capable of resisting the increased horizontal loadings. The shaft is elliptical pre-coloured galvanised steel, offering a muted reflection of the hues of the landscape. The curving top carries the earth cable while the column stem grows minimally out of the ground, bolts and baseplate buried.

The key innovation lies in the principle of the isolator bearings for the conductor lines: all three are set in the same plane and are, for the first time, directed up rather than hung. The suspended isolators can either be composite Neoprene-coated glassfibre or traditional glass. The composite upstanding isolators reduce the height of the pylon – the tallest configuration is 45 metres – and reinforce the idea of flow by allowing the conductors to pass over the cross-arm.

The lily-of-the-valley solution.

CLIENT Electricité de France
COST twice the cost of the present cable pylons
QUANTITY 800 per year

Ian Ritchie/RFR/Kathryn Gustafson 1998

Beyond the périphérique

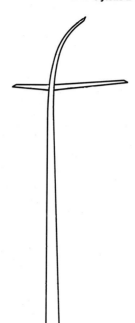

Beyond the périphérique

Ian Ritchie/RFR/Kathryn Gustafson 1998

La Défense

CNIT entrance

The CNIT (National Industrial and Technical Centre) at La Défense was designed as an exhibition hall in 1958 by architects Camerlo, Mailly and Zehrfuss. Pier-Luigi Nervi (1891–1979) engineered the enormous triangular concrete-vault roof, with Jean Prouvé (1901–84) as consultant for the façades. In 1989 the centre was converted (downgraded) into a multi-use convention centre, hotel, shopping mall and office complex, ruining the interior view of the vaults in the process. The new programme required a new 'inviting image' of entrance on the south-west face.

Prouvé was a member of the competition jury for the Centre Pompidou (see page 66) and supported the Rice-Piano-Rogers team's belief that they could get the steelwork built as they had designed it, despite the opposition of the French engineering establishment. To quote Peter Rice, he was 'an untutored, unconventional, maverick engineer and architectural inventor, with an understanding of materials and processes that was precise and unlimiting.'

Prouvé's steel and glass façade (now a loyal replica) is remarkable for its explicitness. Every detail has a specific function, its configuration determined by the way it works. Hung from above, the façade is horizontally braced by the walkways that give access for maintenance and cleaning, all of which can be carried out from the inside. The overlap of structural and programmatic functions in these *passerelles* and in the open glazing of the façade system, which provides both access for the replacing of components and ventilation, is engineering at its best.

RFR tried not to disrupt Prouvé's work but rather to accentuate his ideas. Their new entrance consists of a curved torsion tube cantilevered off the existing concrete columns by steel collars. The existing structure was not conceived to take any additional loads, so work was limited to areas where the framework had reserve capacity. Two glazed canopies

RFR 1992

La Défense

RFR 1992

for terrace cafés (later badly boxed in, undermining the unobtrusive lightness of the design) are fixed to the tube by a fan of steel struts. The variable geometry of the struts is generated by the curve of the tube being projected down to a simple rectangle.

The main entrance is now a lobby air-lock of 'white' glass (fashion technology used without good reason, see the Grande Pyramide, page 18, for its justified use). It is braced by stainless-steel prestressed rod trusses and fixed using an adaptation of the glazing system for the Grandes Serres of the Cité des Sciences et de l'Industrie (see page 230). The structural glazing is over-fussy for the scale of a single-storey entrance addition, throwing into relief the simple elegance of Prouvé's wall. This is not a criticism of one of the most talented design engineering offices in Paris, but a comment on the preponderance of architecturally illiterate clients.

La Défense

ADDRESS La Défense
CLIENT SNC Lucia and SARI Ingénieurie
CONTRACTORS steel, Viry; cable trusses, Sarma; glass, SIV; cladding, Boga
METRO/RER La Défense
ACCESS open

RFR 1992

RFR 1992

Japan Bridge

Having overspilled its original boundary, the boulevard Circulaire, the Parisian business and financial district of La Défense is now expanding westwards towards the suburb of Nanterre. An extraordinary feat of planning has kept the entire area within the boulevard Circulaire as pedestrian only, with all road and rail routes buried underground. Where the roads emerge beyond the Grande Arche (see page 296), two adjacent office blocks have been separated, one inside, one outside the boulevard Circulaire. A footbridge was needed to link them.

Japan Bridge is a stunning tightrope, an aerial speed-stripe 15 metres above the turbulent currents of the traffic below. The bridge spans 100 metres, over seven lanes of carriageway. Perceived at speed by drivers, the Ferrari-red flash shoots across the artery of tail-lights, a rush of adrenaline above the flotsam and jetsam of commerce that laps the edge of Paris.

The steel structure zips out of Kurokawa's semi-cylindrical portal tower. The main arches, welded triangular hollow sections, 900 millimetres wide, were fabricated in five parts – the central section and four legs. Because the façades of the supporting buildings are not parallel, the search for architectural coherence led to an asymmetrical design: one half of the arch is longer than the other. The result is that no two elements have the same length, nor connections the same angle. Computers were essential for the generation of this geometry, for behavioural analysis, and for fabrication.

The inability of the supporting buildings to take significant horizontal thrust caused the bridge to be designed as a tied arch. Consideration of the torsion resulting from the lateral wind load on the walkway glazing led to the double-arch configuration: two bow-string arches leaning together, forming a three-dimensional, stable structure. Arches and

La Défense

Kisho Kurokawa 1992

Kisho Kurokawa 1992

tendons follow parabolic curves, as near funicular as possible to the self-weight of the bridge. The separation of the walkway from the tendon allowed visual emphasis of the tied-arch principle. The walkway is supported on braced struts which spring from the tendons, and is cleaned, carwash-style, by a giant toothbrush.

From the interior of the bridge looking west, Emile Aillaud's towers, late 1960s with tear-shaped windows and pixel camouflage patterns in pastel pinks and purples, promise a certain *Mon Oncle* modernism worthy of closer inspection. However, the sprawling overview from this position suggests something lost. The web of transportation stretches tightly over the landscape with a breed of road-like spaces: railway lines, pipelines, power lines, flight lines. Have we destroyed a sense of place to gain a sense of freedom?

ADDRESS behind the Grande Arche,
cours Valmy, La Défense
CLIENT Sari
CONSULTING ENGINEER Peter Rice: RFR,
with assistance from Ove Arup & Partners
CONTRACTOR Viry SA
BUREAU DE CONTROLE Socotec
METRO/RER La Défense
ACCESS open

Kisho Kurokawa 1992

La Défense

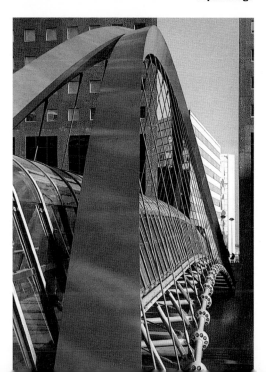

Grande Arche

La Défense is a citadel of skyscrapers, ensnared by roads and rails, outside the Seine and the city proper. Inside the magic circle of the boulevard Circulaire, towers shoot up like beanstalks, some imaginary like Jean Nouvel's Tour Sans Fin, others more concrete, like the giant pinstriped-banker-at-the-disco (1995) by Andrault Parat and Ayoub.

The plan of La Défense is bifurcated by a wide central esplanade. This central mall is strewn with freeform sculptural pieces, the best of which are Takis' tall thin traffic lights. The La Défense esplanade continues the Le Nôtre axis. The trajectory of this route started with Le Nôtre's perspective from the Louvre and Tuileries Gardens (1664) to the *allée perspective* of the Champs-Elysées. This linear organisation of points and planes came, until recently, to a visual halt at the Arc de Triomphe (1806–36). Today, standing at place Charles-de-Gaulle, formerly place de l'Etoile, from which 12 broad avenues radiate to create a star shape, it is possible to see the Grande Pyramide of the Louvre in one direction and the Grande Arche of La Défense in the other.

The problem of how to end a perspective and yet leave your options open for future continuation is have-your-cake-and-eat-it challenge. And because you go through or under arches, they set up an expectation that something will happen next. Ever since the Arc de Triomphe was built there has been a notion that the view away from the centre should be terminated somehow. After several rehearsals in the 1970s, when various schemes for this resolution were commissioned and abandoned, Mitterrand set up an international competition. There were 424 entries.

The givens and results of the competition, won by von Sprekelsen, bear an extraordinary similarity to the story of Jørn Utzon and the Sydney Opera House. Both were international competitions for peninsular sites. Both demanded a landmark building, a symbol for a major city. Both were

Johann-Otto von Sprekelsen, Paul Andreu 1989

La Défense

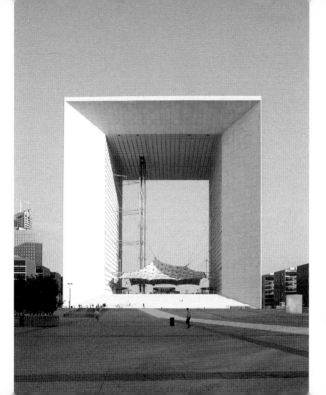

won by unknown Danish men who had produced expressive sketches. Both architects ran into trouble and broke their contracts, leaving their buildings to be completed by others. While Utzon left Sydney and never returned to see his building finished, von Sprekelsen left the Grande Arche in ill health and died before it was completed. Both projects were supported by engineers Ove Arup & Partners, with Peter Rice: at the age of 26, the opera house was Rice's first major job; at 52, the Nuages for the Grande Arche was one of his last.

There is a simplicity and purity about von Sprekelsen's idea. An almost perfect cube, the arch is Palladian rather than Platonic, its form suggesting a geometric timelessness and monumentality, not least because of its huge size. The ambiguity of whether it is a 'window' to look through or a 'door' to pass through is part of its intrigue. Perhaps this question will be resolved when the next landmark object arrives on the axis.

The structure is simple: a giant egg crate supported on Neoprene cushions on six rows of piles. The complex of tunnels under the site meant piles could not be driven in exactly on the grand axis. As a result, the arch has a 6.5-degree inflection to the north, which echoes the inflected angle of the Louvre at the other end of the route. Before construction started, Mitterrand tested its full-scale presence by having four helicopters hover at its proposed height while he stood watching from the Louvre.

On either side of the arch are Les Collines, office blocks designed by Buffi and Lenormand, 1990, added by the developers to make the whole package commercially viable. The arch itself is a banal container of offices (south side, government ministries; north side, private companies) detailed with the slickness of an airport development, a big building with the predictable belvedere on top reached by glass lifts.

La Défense

Johann-Otto von Sprekelsen, Paul Andreu 1989

Johann-Otto von Sprekelsen, Paul Andreu 1989

The geometry of the arch cannot be isolated from its sensual qualities, in particular its use of light (von Sprekelsen's work previous to the Grande Arche commission had amounted to four churches). He envisaged the arch as a monolith around which more 'ephemeral things' would happen. These were constructed in a literal way from sketches after his death as the Nuages (clouds) within the arch.

The Nuages is a structure in fabric, steel and glass suspended in the volume of the Grande Arche to give it scale and measure. It was designed and engineered by Peter Rice working with Paul Andreu, who succeeded von Sprekelsen as architect to the project. As the Teflon fabric of which it is made is only faintly translucent, the quality of lightness is difficult to perceive. In order to recreate the three-dimensional presence of clouds from flat fabric, an undulating surface was used. Peter Rice: 'It is supported on radiating cable trusses so that the real volume occupied by the fabric was joined by the virtual volume of the steel structure giving a large presence in the space.'

Von Sprekelsen's project for the Grand Arche envisaged the Nuages as fluid, freeform layers spilling out over the esplanade in strong contrast with the monolithic building. A sinusoidal module was created which could be connected to itself in several ways, allowing a multitude of different shapes, all sharing a character which flows from the geometry of the basic unit, to be formed. This flowing dimension was never realised.

The ephemerality of the project is a result of the way the building receives light. The pilgrimage up the monumental stair suggests one is approaching an altar to the sun or moon. The most important material is the white Carrara marble that covers the splayed walls and steps (the architects of Venice similarly used white stone window frames to help bounce light from the narrow streets into the interior spaces).

La Défense

Johann-Otto von Sprekelsen, Paul Andreu 1989

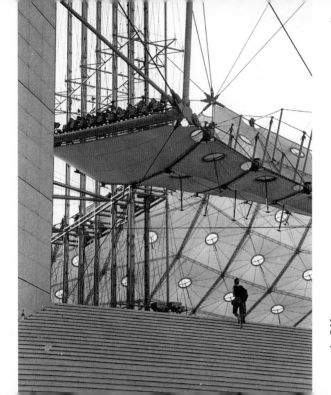

Von Sprekelsen's idea for the arch was painterly rather than sculptural. Where a painting on a two-dimensional surface can allude to the three dimensional, he has taken the three-dimensional space of the building and is alluding to the space beyond that: 'a view to the future' in the freest sense. The light is used materially, and is presenceful; the arch is not empty, it is a space solid with light.

ADDRESS La Défense
CLIENT Société d'Economie Mixte Tête-Défense
CONSULTING ENGINEERS Ove Arup & Partners, Peter Rice
SIZE 110 x 103 x 111 metres; offices 115,000 square metres
METRO/RER La Défense
ACCESS belvedere open 8.00–19.00

Johann-Otto von Sprekelsen, Paul Andreu 1989

La Défense

La Défense

Johann-Otto von Sprekelsen, Paul Andreu 1989

Index

Paris: a guide to recent architecture

Paris: a guide to recent architecture

Paris: a guide to recent architecture

Paris: a guide to recent architecture

Paris: a guide to recent architecture

Paris: a guide to recent architecture

Paris: a guide to recent architecture

Paris: a guide to recent architecture